燕园珍藏

王恩哥 主编

北京大学出版社
PEKING UNIVERSITY PRESS

序

任北京大学校长期间，我代表学校赠予来宾最多的两本书是《燕园草木》和《走进北大》。前一本书的作者是老校长许智宏先生，后一本是我2013年倡议并主持编写的。这段时间，我走遍了校园的每个角落，时常为燕园曲折丰饶的历史人文积淀所感叹。从那时起，我就有一个心愿：在离开校长岗位后，把北大珍藏的瑰宝汇集成一本册子，以展现这所百年学府的底蕴与魅力。这个想法得到了许多朋友的支持。

细数北大一百二十年变迁沉淀的珍藏，犹如散布各处的珍珠，璀璨夺目，俯拾即是。然而将这些珍贵的遗存与记忆搜集整理成册又谈何容易。从最初提出想法到大纲落定，就花去了两年时间，期间我们又听取了许多专家学者的建议。正是集大家之力，才使这本书雏形渐现。

本书分为四部分。开篇首章为"历史的记忆"，主要展示北大百余年来校史与校园的重要印迹。第二章为"知识的传承"，意在记录燕园这片土地上不同领域的学者们对人类知识边界与高度的挑战。第三章是"自然的馈赠"，精选燕园所珍藏的珍贵地质标本和植物样本。最后一章为"文明的守护"，是中华文明与文化千百年来沉淀于燕园的一些最具代表与特色的呈现。

在我眼中，天下风景，唯燕园最美。其美不单单在于一片独特潇逸的校园。正如谢冕先生所言，燕园其实不大，未名不过一勺水。然而，这片土地上遍布着让人惊喜的发现。燕园之美，更在于身处其中所能触摸和感受到的一种无形魅力的浸

Preface 序

染——尽管人们很难准确形容这是一种什么精神，但它就在那里。每一个北大人，每一位生活在这片土地上的人都有自己内心的解读。

燕园珍藏，是燕园之美的集中体现。无论是钟灵毓秀的湖光塔影，还是救亡图存的一声呐喊，无论是知识探索的寂寞与坚守，还是自然与文明的眷顾和恩赐，从任何一个角度来看，燕园都充满着一种独特的美的气质，凝聚着北大人从未停止的对美的信仰和追求。

燕园珍藏，贵在于大。很少有一所大学能拥有如此庞大的珍藏体系和资源。历史与校园、智慧与创新、自然与文明，但凡我们能想象到有关珍藏的分类尺度，都在这片物理空间不过三四千亩的土地上得到呼应。更难能可贵的是，这些珍藏无形之中透出一种宏大的气象。没有故步自封，没有畏缩迟疑，没有自娱自乐，而总是以心怀天下、学至精微为最基本的关怀。

燕园珍藏，重在于精。如果要将燕园的珍藏一一列入名录，那恐怕写一本百科全书都难以尽揽。故我们只能从浩如烟海的精品中择其精要，将一些从不同角度代表北大的故事整理成册献给大家。我相信，这是一个真实的燕园，一个厚重的燕园，一个在他处永远不可复制的燕园。

在编著这本书的过程中，我常常想到，一个人的强大不在于征服了什么，而在于为道路和坚守承受了什么。一所大学历经风雨所承载的历史与文化，不也正是其如此厚重、如此卓越的一种体现吗？

大学，有精神方成气象，有血脉故能传承。希望这本册子能带给每个人关于燕园美的享受，形成读者心中对于燕园一份独特的珍藏。

是为序。

北京大学原校长
中国科学院副院长、院士　　王恩哥

2017年年末于朗润园

Preface

During my tenure as the President of Peking University (PKU), the two books that I most often presented to visitors were *Yan Yuan Horticulture* and *Exploring Peking University*, which organized and edited by former PKU President Xu Zhihong and myself, respectively. Over the years, every time I strolled around the campus, I was struck by its beauty and culture. Always I felt a lingering wish to publish a book about the treasures of PKU, sharing the University's cultural heritage, the intellectual depth of its pursuits, and the aesthetic beauty of the grounds. When I expressed my idea to friends and colleagues, they encouraged me to proceed.

The treasures of PKU, accumulated over its long history, are enormous; hence I knew it would be impossible to include all of them in a single volume. Even with the concerted effort of a team of many friends, it still took more than two years to get from the idea's inception to the final product.

There are four chapters in this book: Chapter One, Historical Memories, follows the footprints of PKU history. Chapter Two, Knowledge Inheritance, describes the deep intellectual tradition of PKU scholars in pushing the boundaries of knowledge and challenging the world with innovative ideas. Chapter Three, Gifts from Nature, describes some rare natural specimens housed at PKU. Chapter Four, Safeguard of Civilization, reflects a crystallization and representation of Chinese culture and civilization reflected in the PKU collection.

The elegance of PKU, according to Professor Xie Mian, lies not only in its charming lake and peaceful gardens, but also in the material and spiritual treasures that one cannot avoid seeing when crossing the campus. These treasures are incarnated in a transcendental beauty that is impossible to describe in words, and yet inescapably felt in the hearts of PKU alumni and visitors.

Preface 序

The treasures of PKU—the beautiful lake and garden, the humanity and patriotism demonstrated during the World Wars, the passionate pursuit of knowledge, the heritage of culture and nature, all endowed this campus and its people with a unique character and aesthetics that have driven them to pursue truth and beauty unrelentingly throughout the years.

The number of treasures is so large that only a handful of the world's universities can compete. Furthermore, the value of these treasures is priceless. There is hardly any self-indulgence, self-congratulation, or arrogance; instead, reflected in them is a deep and passionate appreciation of the most fundamental aspects of the world, a *pro bono humani generis*.

Listing all the treasures would require many volumes. Therefore, we painstakingly selected only a small percentage of items that are the most representative ones. I sincerely hope the entries in this book will introduce readers to PKU's great heritage, which is irreplaceable.

In editing this book, I came to realize that a person's power is not reflected by what he conquers, but rather, by what he endures and upholds along an arduous journey. Similarly, isn't it also true that a university's excellence is reflected in its culture and history, the glorious as well as the trying.

This university has a grand tradition built on a solid philosophical foundation, nurtured by impressive intellectual achievements. As such, it has made an enormous impact not just on China itself, but the whole world. We hope our readers gain some of the appreciation for PKU that we, the authors, felt in writing this book.

Enge Wang
President Emeritus, Peking University
Vice President and Academician,
Chinese Academy of Sciences
Langrunyuan, December of 2017

目录
Contents

第一章　历史的记忆
Chapter One　Historical Memories　/ 1

1.1 旧园寻踪
1.1 Pursuing the Traces of the Old Gardens　/ 4

1.2 燕大新规
1.2 The New Constructions in Yenching University　/ 26

1.3 圆明园遗珍
1.3 Relics of the Old Summer Palace　/ 54

1.4 建筑小品
1.4 Architectural Oddments　/ 68

第二章　知识的传承
Chapter Two　Knowledge Inheritance　/ 81

2.1 校风传承
2.1 Inheritance of School Spirits　/ 84

2.2 知识创新
2.2 Knowledge Innovation　/ 98

第三章　自然的馈赠
Chapter Three　Gifts from Nature　/ 133

3.1 地质标本
3.1 Geological Specimens　/ 136

3.2 植物样本
3.2 Plant Samples　/ 156

第四章　文明的守护
Chapter Four　Safeguard of Civilization　/ 167

4.1 文物聚珍
4.1 Collections of Cultural Relics　/ 170

4.2 古籍善本
4.2 Chinese Rare Book Collection　/ 186

4.3 金石拓本
4.3 Epigraphy Section　/ 226

4.4 艺术精品
4.4 Treasures of Art　/ 236

后记
Epilogue　/ 250

Chapter One
Historical Memories

第一章
历史的记忆

明清时期，皇家和大臣纷纷在西山附近修筑园林。在现今北京大学的范围内，先后有勺园、畅春园、淑春园、鸣鹤园、镜春园、朗润园、治贝子园、蔚秀园和承泽园等著名园林。这些园林保存状况不一，有的仅余空名，引后人遐思，有的则保留了较多的形胜供游人欣赏。这些园林中，最早的是明代著名艺术家米万钟修建的勺园，最为著名的是在淑春园基础上发展而来的现未名湖景区。这些明清园林为20世纪20年代燕京大学的建设提供了良好的环境，燕京大学围绕湖区建设了主校区。2001年，"未名湖燕园建筑"被列为全国重点文物保护单位。现在，未名湖景区是北京大学最吸引人的风景区，学生们将未名湖、博雅塔、图书馆亲切地称为"一塔湖图"。

未名湖畔
The Weiming Lake (the So-called Unnamed Lake)

Chapter One: Historical Memories
第一章 历史的记忆

The imperial families and officials of the Ming and Qing Dynasties were keen on building private gardens in places adjacent to the Western Hills, Beijing. The campus of Peking University occupies a zone where some famous gardens used to or still sit in, including the Shaoyuan (Shao Garden), Changchunyuan (Changchun Garden), Shuchunyuan (Shuchun Garden), Mingheyuan (Minghe Garden), Jingchunyuan (Jingchun Garden), Langrunyuan (Langrun Garden), Zhibeiziyuan (Prince Zhi's Garden), Weixiuyuan (Weixiu Garden) and Chengzeyuan (Chengze Garden). Some have long gone and only their names have survived. Others have been better preserved and become places of interest. Among the above-listed gardens, the Shaoyuan built by Mi Wanzhong, a renowned Ming artist has been the earliest one, and the Shuchunyuan has been the best-known, for the Weiming Lake (the so-called Unnamed Lake) scenic area is developed upon it. These Ming and Qing gardens prepared attractive environments for Yenching University in the 1920s, the main campus of which was built around the Weiming Lake. In 2001, "the Architectural Complex of Yan Yuan by the Weiming Lake" in Peking University was inscribed on the list of State Priority Protection Sites. The Weiming Lake area is the most attractive part on the campus of Peking University. Students call the Weiming Lake, Boya Pagoda and the library "Yi Ta Hu Tu", humorously and affectionately a homonym of "a total mess" in Chinese, while in reality a name of affection that can be translated as "a scroll painting of the lakeside pagoda and library".

1.1 旧园寻踪
1.1 Pursuing the Traces of the Old Gardens

1.1.1 恩佑寺、恩慕寺山门

畅春园是清圣祖康熙皇帝在北京西北郊建造的一座"避喧听政"的皇家园林，由此开启了海淀附近清代皇家园林开辟和营造的宏阔历史。今天，除残余恩佑寺和恩慕寺山门之外，畅春园昔日盛况早已杳然无踪。其旧址大致在今北大西墙之外，蔚秀园和承泽园以南，西至万泉河路西侧，南至双桥东路一线。20 世纪 80 年代时，北大购入了畅春园故址的东北部分，使得校园内又增加了一座旧日园林。

恩佑寺、恩慕寺山门皆坐西朝东，相距十余米。两门大小规格基本相同，均为单檐歇山黄琉璃顶，下辟砖石拱券，不用斗拱。檐下嵌有石匾，上分别刻有"敬建恩佑寺""敬建恩慕寺"，前者居北，为雍正皇帝御笔；后者居南，为乾隆皇帝御笔。

恩佑寺原为康熙年间的清溪书屋，后在雍正元年改为恩佑寺，以纪念康熙皇帝。恩慕寺则是乾隆四十二年，乾隆皇帝为了纪念去世的孝圣皇太后而建。

Chapter One: Historical Memories
第一章 历史的记忆

恩慕寺山门（摄影/何晋）
The Gate of En Mu Temple (Photography by He Jin)

1.1.1 The Gate of En You Temple and the Gate of En Mu Temple

　　Changchunyuan is an imperial garden built by Emperor Kangxi (r. 1661 – 1722) in the northwest of Beijing to "avoiding noises and handling the governmental affairs", thus promoting the establishment and construction of royal gardens in Haidian District during Qing Dynasty. Today, except the Gate of En You Temple and the Gate of En Mu Temple, the grandeur of Changchunyuan exists in name only. The former site roughly borders Weixiuyuan and Chengzeyuan on the north, Wanquanhe Road on the west, Shuangqiao East Road on the south and the west wall of Peking University. Peking University purchased

恩佑寺山门（摄影 / 何晋）
The Gate of En You Temple (Photography by He Jin)

the northeast part of Changchunyuan in the 1980s, which added an old-timey garden to the campus.

Both gates of En You Temple and En Mu Temple face the east, and they are about ten meters apart. Their sizes and specifications are almost the same, which have single eave roof with yellow roof tiles and have an arch of bricks and stone below without bracket system. Under the eaves lie stone tablets on which carved the name of the temple—"Jingjian En You Temple" (*Jingjian* means to build with great respect) written by Emperor Yongzheng (r. 1723 – 1735), and "Jingjian En Mu Temple" written by Emperor Qianlong (r. 1735 – 1796). En You Temple is on the north of the En Mu Temple.

The En You Temple was built as a reading room called Qingxi Shuwu (Limpid Stream Study) in Kangxi period, and was later changed into the En You Temple by Emperor Qianlong in his 1st year of reign in memory of Emperor Kangxi. As for the En Mu Temple, it was built by Emperor Qianlong in memory of his mother Empress Dowager Xiaosheng.

1.1.2 乾隆诗碑

乾隆诗碑位于北大未名湖西侧南岸，蔡元培先生铜像东侧，是北大的著名景观。乾隆诗碑长约两米，高约一米，碑前后两面均有乾隆御笔，此碑为畅春园之遗物。

诗作于乾隆五十二年，记乾隆十三、十四年之事。十三年九月，"诣畅春园恭皇太后圣安，即视事于观澜榭，引见于大西门""爱亲御弧矢""连发二十矢，中一十有九"，十四年，"陈马技以娱慈颜，亲发十矢，复中九，且破其的三焉"。

乾隆诗碑
Qianlong's Royal Poem Tablet

Chapter One: Historical Memories
第一章 历史的记忆

1.1.2 Qianlong's Royal Poem Tablet

As one of the most significant sights in Peking University, Emperor Qianlong's Royal Poem Tablet is located on southwest bank of Weiming Lake, just to the east of Bronze Statue of Cai Yuanpei (1868 – 1940). The tablet with Qianlong's writing on both sides is a relic from the Old Summer Palace. And it is two meters in length, one meter in height.

These two poems were composed in the 52nd year of Qianlong (1787) to remember affairs happened in the 13th and 14th year of Qianlong.

In September of the 13th year of Qianlong's period, the emperor "paid a visit to Empress Dowager in Changchunyuan, deal with political affairs in Guanlanxie and meet courtiers at the Grand West Gate" "draw the bow and shoot arrows in succession, hitting nineteen targets out of twenty". In the 14th year of Qianlong, he "rid the horse to entertain the Empress dowager, hitting nine targets out of ten, including three at the bull's eyes".

乾隆诗碑
Qianlong's Royal Poem Tablet

1.1.3 校景亭

校景亭，原名翼然亭，亭如其名，檐飞翘向上，泰然与动势并举，是燕园里最古老的亭。乾隆曾登临翼然亭观赏，作《翼然亭》诗以记其事，前有序云："出西轩面横岭，亭中设便坐，近纳岚翠，远往野绿，仿佛香山来青景色。"诗曰：

> 峰有飞来亭岂无，
> 天然距此不甯图。
> 藉松为幄阴偏秀，
> 倚石成章兴迥殊。
> 茶鼎烟飞云半野，
> 棋枰声杂瀑千株。
> 寄言纵目搜吟客，
> 莫认琅邪岩畔途。

1926 年，燕京大学建校，对其进行修缮，将校园内代表性的景色绘于亭上，此亭遂被称为校景亭。

1.1.3 The Pavilion of Campus Scenery

Formerly named Yiran Pavilion, the Pavilion of Campus Scenery has curved eaves just as its name. It has not only a static beauty, but also a dynamic beauty. The Pavilion of Campus Scenery is the oldest pavilion in Yan Yuan.

Emperor Qianlong once went sightseeing in this pavilion, and wrote a poem about his journey. And the preface of the poem says:

> *Walking out of the west veranda and facing Mount Hengling, a seat is set up in the pavilion, The woods are lovely, wild and deep, reminding me of the Laiqingxuan on the Fragrant Hill.*

The poem is as follow:

Like Fei Lai Feng in the south, the pavilion seems like as if it could fly.
Look no further than here, since Fei Lai Feng is far away in the south
Engulfed by the shadows of the pine trees,
Leaning against the rocks, I write a poem in different moods.
The smoke from the tea arises creep into the clouds,
The sound of colliding chesses is mixed with the tumbling waterfall.
I cast about for the traces of the poets,
Don't let the rocks hinder you.

When Yenching University was established in 1926, the pavilion was repaired and the representative scenes throughout the campus were painted on the pavilion. Since then it was called the Pavilion of Campus Scenery.

校景亭
The Pavilion of Campus Scenery

1.1.4 原燕京大学未名湖区

　　未名湖景区原属于清代淑春园，基本保存了淑春园的山形水系，还有石舫等淑春园旧物。

　　在淑春园为燕大辟为校址后，园中又添置了不少点缀校园的文物或者景观——如翻尾石鱼、四扇屏、斯诺墓等，为燕园增添了不少景致。

　　据载，淑春园曾由乾隆赐给和珅。和珅拥有淑春园后，除了在园中点缀一湖一岛以仿圆明园外，还在园中添置了一座石舫。这座石舫，今天仍保留了石质基座，横卧在未名湖中，这也是淑春园中留下的一件旧物。

　　除未名湖的石舫外，今天在颐和园、圆明园等处也保留有石舫。咸丰十年英法联军火烧圆明园，淑春园亦遭破坏，仅残存石舫底座及"临风待月楼"，即今临湖轩故址。

未名湖景区
Weiming Lake Area

1.1.4 Weiming Lake Area in Yenching University

The Weiming Lake Area belonged to Shuchunyuan in Qing Dynasty. The landform of Shuchunyuan was mostly preserved along with the relics of the garden like the Marble Boat and so on.

Many new relics and landscape pieces such as the Roll-Tailed Stone Fish, the Four Stone Tablets, the Tomb of Snow and so on have been placed to embellish the campus since the garden was changed into the campus of Yenching University.

Emperor Qianlong granted the garden as a reward to He Shen. He Shen imitated the Old Summer Palace by making a lake and an islet in the garden and also placed a marble boat after the grant from Emperor Qianlong. The base of the marble boat was still lying in the Weiming Lake, which was also one of the remaining relics of the garden.

石舫
Marble Boat

Treasures of Yan Yuan
燕园珍藏

Chapter One: Historical Memories
第一章　历史的记忆

石舫
Marble Boat

Besides the marble boat in Weiming Lake, there are marble boats in the Summer Palace, the Old Summer Palace and some other places. Shuchunyuan was destroyed when British and French expeditionary forces set fire to the Old Summer Palace in the 10th year of Emperor Xianfeng's reign. Only the base of the marble boat and a building called "Lin Feng Dai Yue Lou" (the building of facing wind and waiting for the moon) left. The building was once located at where the present Linhuxuan (Lake House) stands.

1.1.5 后湖

未名湖北二三百米，即是镜春园和朗润园。环绕穿插两园之间的，是被称作"后湖"的一片水系。这片清流环绕、宁静致远的后湖区域，曾是季羡林、金克木、邓广铭、张中行、钱穆、宗白华、陈岱孙、叶企孙、汤一介等许多著名学者居住、生活的地方。20 世纪 90 年代，由于地下水位下降和环境变化，失去水源的后湖逐年干涸、荒草丛生，曾经生机盎然的湖区逐渐凋零。何日再有源头活水，使后湖景观再现，成为很多北大人的企盼。

2013 年，学校决定实施"燕园景观与环境综合整治"总体规划方案，以实现水资源的循环利用，践行"绿色校园"理念，推动环境育人。修复驳岸，疏浚河道，建设中水站，引水入园，处理后的中水从荷花湖源源不断地流向未名湖和后湖。短短几年变迁，今日再次漫步后湖，春可观野鸭游弋、鸳鸯戏水，夏可赏红荷映日、荇菜参差，秋冬之际，师生们依旧偏爱这"水木明瑟，曲径通幽"的世外桃源。这里已然成为许多北大师生散步休憩、放飞思绪的去处，就连许多小动物也"慕名前来"，在此安家。人与自然的重逢，让这片古朴静谧的土地重新焕发了勃勃生机。

后湖改造前照片
Pictures Taken Before the Rear Lake was Renovated

Chapter One: Historical Memories
第一章　历史的记忆

后湖改造后照片
Pictures Taken after the Rear Lake Came Back to Life

后湖改造后照片
Pictures Taken after the Rear Lake Came Back to Life

1.1.5 Rear Lake

Two or three hundred meters to the north of the Weiming Lake, lies the Rear Lake, or Houhu in Chinese. Adjacent to the Jingchunyuan and Langrunyuan, the Rear Lake is known for its tranquil charm, where some well-known scholars such as Ji Xianlin, Jin Kemu, Deng Guangming, Zhang Zhongxing, Qian Mu, Zong Baihua, Chen Daisun, Ye Qisun and Tang Yijie had lived. In the 1990s, the Rear Lake dried up due to the drop of groundwater level and environmental changes. Afterwards, it became a popular hope to restore the natural beauty someday.

In 2013, Peking University decided to implement the overall landscape upgrade plan and bring back the missing scenes of the campus, the Rear Lake being a key project. With much effort, the lake came back to life once again. In recent years, people like taking a stroll along the winding paths to free up one's mind by the peaceful lake, with wild lotus blooming and ducks playing in the water. The Rear Lake nowadays is not only a favorite spot for people but also home for numerous animals. The reunion of man and nature has revived this peaceful land once again.

后湖改造后照片
Pictures Taken after the Rear Lake Came Back to Life

Chapter One: Historical Memories
第一章 历史的记忆

野鸭在成片的荇菜中穿行
Wild Ducks Swimming Through the Cress

夜鹭在后湖捕鱼
Night Heron Fishing in the Lake

后湖改造后照片
Pictures Taken after the Rear Lake Came Back to Life

1.1.6 花神庙

花神庙位于未名湖南岸,原来是慈济寺的山门,不知何故得此名称。进入山门拾级而上,有一座向北的正殿和东、西配殿,现在正殿的殿址就是斯诺墓碑所在的地方。

花神庙
Flora Temple

1.1.6 Flora Temple

Located on the south bank of the Weiming Lake, it was once the gate of Ci Ji Temple, which somehow was nicknamed the Flora Temple. Through the gate and up the steps, there was a compound of halls. The main hall of the temple faced the north while the other two halls stood respectively on the sides of east and west. Now the site of the main hall of the temple is where Edgar Snow's tomb lies.

花神庙
Flora Temple

1.2 燕大新规

1.2 The New Constructions in Yenching University

1.2.1 老规划图中的早期燕园景观

燕园风景绝胜。湖光塔影，雕梁画栋，常与颐和园、圆明园等并列，被认为反映了古典皇家园林的风貌。事实上，这是一个有趣的误会。

燕园所处之地虽曾为皇家园林，但历经清季民初兵燹，已大抵片瓦无存。今天的燕园，自20世纪20年代初由美国建筑师亨利·墨菲主持营建，经由初期在设计思想、功能布局、建筑形式以及建造预算等多方面的冲突和妥协，至1926年夏，已初具今日未名湖区的面貌。北大校档案馆藏这一时期的《燕京大学一览》即反映了此时的校园景观。未名湖，博雅塔，办公楼群，德、才、均、备斋，静园，南北阁，一、二体育馆以及燕南园、燕东园等，均已初具形态，而细节又与今日多有不同。例如，图中的静园有十二个院落，现实中仅陆续建成六个；花神庙遗迹计划被一座男生宿舍楼所取代，而最终得以保全；图中的学生中心、男生食堂等建筑则从未建成。方案的建筑形式借鉴了中国传统样式，而其基本景观格局，如轴线布置、三合构成、几何形绿地等，则明显脱胎于传统的西方大学校园，显示出浓厚的美国影响。在此

Chapter One: Historical Memories
第一章 历史的记忆

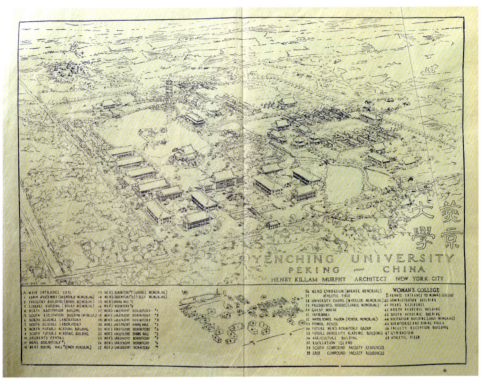

燕京大学规划图（1926年）
Campus Plans of Yenching University (1926)

后的长期校园建设实践中，方案中的不切实际与不合文脉之处被陆续矫正，燕园遂逐渐被建设为中西合璧、古今融合的校园景观瑰宝。

1.2.1 Campus Landscape in Archived Early Campus Plans

The campus of Peking University is located in an area filled with former imperial gardens in the Qing Dynasty. With the beautiful traditional Chinese style architecture, and pagoda, and the lake, the campus, along with the old and new Summer Palaces, is commonly imagined as one of the most iconic works of China's imperial gardening art. Nevertheless, this image is somewhat misleading.

Despite the once existence of the gardens, they had been mostly demolished in the turmoil in the downfall of the Qing Dynasty, and left little physical legacy to today's PKU campus landscape. The campus, as it is today, was mostly the design of a New York architect, Henry Murphy, based on his sometimes inaccurate understandings of traditional Chinese art of architecture. The implementation of the architect's design, however, had

Chapter One: Historical Memories
第一章 历史的记忆

never been easy. Culture conflicts, technical difficulties, and budget constrains prevailed the early days of the construction of the campus. Nevertheless, after a series of conflicts and compromise, by summer 1926, the campus landscape, which was preserved in the *Bird-eye View of Yenching University* kept in the Archives of PKU, had already been quite recognizable to today's observers. The lake, the pagoda, and the main buildings were all in similar shapes as what they are today, but were different in certain details. For example, the Jingyuan had twelve courts in the map, but in reality only four had been built by 1926, and six by today; the student center and men's dining hall in the map have never been built until today. Overall, the map features Chinese style architecture, but Western style landscaping techniques as revealed in the main axis, the courts, and the geometrical greens. With the continuous efforts of generations of campus builders since, the combination of the styles of the two cultures turns out to be a success, and the campus has thus become a masterpiece of modern China campus landscape.

燕大初期建筑群
Campus Landscape of Yenching University

1.2.2 西校门、石狮及校友桥

　　西校门为北京大学的正门，坐东朝西。在墨菲的设计中，西校门位于燕园的主轴线起点。墨菲以玉泉山的古塔作为端点，向东延伸作为校园的主轴线，由此确定了西校门的位置。这样他就一反北京坐北朝南的传统，设计燕园的主校门面朝西布置。进入西校门，通过校友桥，正对着校园的主要建筑——办公楼，再穿过未名湖，

Chapter One: Historical Memories
第一章 历史的记忆

直至东端的博雅塔，这些景致都在校园的主轴线上。

西校门在燕京大学时期是燕园的正门，当时门正中悬挂着由蔡元培先生手书的"燕京大学"四字匾额。1952年，北京大学迁入燕园以后，门正中换上了"北京大学"四字匾额。"北京大学"四字是由毛泽东主席在1950年应北大学生会的请求亲笔题写的，与红色的校门浑然一体。

西校门石狮是燕京大学于1924年从民间购得，在北大校档案馆里，还存有当时购买这对石狮的契据。

西校门
West Gate

Treasures of Yan Yuan
燕园珍藏

校友桥与西校门同时建造于 1926 年，由校友捐款修建，故名"校友桥"。进入西门便见此桥，位于校园的主干道上，引领着人们走向办公楼。它是燕园中最大的桥。

石狮
Stone Lion

1.2.2 West Gate, Stone Lions and Alumni Bridge

The West Gate facing the west is the main gate of Peking University. It was designed to be the starting point of the main axis by Henry K. Murphy. He drew a line from the ancient pagoda on the Jade Spring Hill to form the main axis of the campus; thus confirmed the location of the West Gate. However, the design that the West Gate should face the west instead of the south went against the traditions in Beijing. Through the gate and the Alumni Bridge there was the Administrative Building, the main building on the campus. And through the Weiming Lake stands the Boya Pagoda at eastern end of the central axis. All these buildings mentioned above should be on the main axis.

The West Gate was the former main entrance of Yenching University. A horizontally inscribed board with characters of "Yan Jing Da Xue" (Yenching University), written by Cai Yuanpei, was hung in the middle of the lintel of the West Gate. In 1952, the inscription on horizontally inscribed board was changed into "Bei Jing Da Xue" (Peking University) when Peking University moved into Yan Yuan. These four characters were written by Chairman Mao Zedong upon the request of the student union of Peking University in 1950. The board matches well with the red gate.

The stone lions were purchased from market by Yenching University. There is still the receipt in the Archives of Peking University.

The Alumni Bridge was built along with the school gate of Yenching University in 1926. And it was given this name because of the donation from university alumni. It was directed towards the West Gate, and was located on the main road, leading people to the Administrative Building. Besides, it was the largest bridge in Yan Yuan.

Treasures of Yan Yuan
燕园珍藏

Chapter One: Historical Memories
第一章 历史的记忆

校友桥
The Alumni Bridge

1.2.3 办公楼

办公楼建于 1926 年,原名"施德楼",仿中国传统建筑风格,依清代宫殿式建筑为蓝本设计。1931 年 6 月燕京大学校楼命名委员会曾定名为"贝公楼"。现在是北大校领导办公的地方。

楼体位于未名湖古建筑区中轴线上。两边的外文楼、化学北楼(现名大雅堂)与办公楼呈品字形排列,对称布局。放弃规划时四合院的组合形式,而采取开放的三合院布局,突显了拥有高台基的办公楼的大气,也与其后树丛掩映中的未名湖区的园林雅趣形成了鲜明的对比。

办公楼
Administrative Building

1.2.3 Administrative Building

Completed in 1926, the Administrative Building was originally named as Shide Building, which was an intimation of Chinese traditional architecture. It modeled the palatial architecture of Qing Dynasty. In June 1931, it was renamed Beigong Building by the Building Designation Committee, Yenching University. Now it is named Administrative Building, where the Office of the President of Peking University is.

The building is on the central axis of the ancient architecture around Weiming Lake. Administrative Building, with the symmetrically arranged the Foreign Language Building and the Chemistry Building, together form a layout just like the shape of Chinese character "品". It chooses the three-section compound instead of the four-section courtyard compound as usually planned in Beijing area, which makes the Administrative Building on the high pedestal more impressive and stands in sharp contrast to the elegant gardens around Weiming Lake behind the building.

办公楼
Administrative Building

1.2.4 临湖轩

临湖轩是清朝乾隆年间权臣和珅位于淑春园的"临风待月楼"的遗址，1860年淑春园被毁时只有未名湖边的石舫基座和这座楼保存下来。燕大建校时，时任校长司徒雷登的费城友人捐资修缮此楼，赠给校长司徒雷登作为住宅。1931年根据冰心提议将其命名为"临湖轩"。马寅初任北大校长期间（1951—1960年）也曾在此居住，现为北大贵宾接待室。临湖轩西北有山林环抱，东北可眺山色湖光，南有竹林作屏障，东临幽谷深池，环境清幽。此处依山就势，高低错落，远观只见屋脊，入内则别有天地。

临湖轩
Linhuxuan (Lake House)

1.2.4 Lake House

Lake House stands on the site of "Lin Feng Dai Yue Lou" (the building of facing wind and waiting for the moon) in Shuchunyuan of He Shen, a powerful official in the reign of Emperor Qianlong. When the garden was destroyed in 1860, only "Lin Feng Dai Yue Lou" and the base of the marble boat remain. When Yenching University was established, friends of John Leighton Stuart, who was the president of Yenching University at that time, funded to restore the building and gave it to President Stuart as his residence. In 1931, it was renamed as "Lake House" following the advice of Bing Xin, a well-known female writer. After 1949, Ma Yinchu, former president of Peking University, once lived here. Today, Lake House is used as the reception room to receive the foreign visitors, including government leaders, experts and scholars. At the northwest of the building, there are the hills and forests embracing the building. And people could overlook landscape of lake and hill at the direction of northeast. With a pool lying at the east side, the building is hidden in the bamboo groves in the south. The building was constructed according to typology. And one could only see the roof of the building, but will find ample spaces and unique scenery if they get into the yard.

早期临湖轩
The Lake House in its Early Time

1.2.5 博雅塔

博雅塔取法通州燃灯塔，但却作为一座水塔使用。由燕大哲学系教授博晨光的叔父捐资兴建，故名"博雅"。

燕园的设计者墨菲认为，"塔是中国最具象征性和最具特色的人造景观"，在墨菲的规划中突显出对塔的钟爱。虽然当时关于在园林中建塔是否合适有过激烈的争论，但校方最终还是采纳了墨菲的方案。

1.2.5 Boya Pagoda

Imitated from the ancient "Ran Deng Pagoda"(Light-igniting Pagoda) in the city of Tongzhou, Boya Pagoda was used as a water tower. It was given the name "Boya" in honor of the donor, the uncle of Lucius. C. Porter who was a professor of the Department of Philosophy, Yenching University.

Henry K. Murphy, the designer of Yan Yuan thought that pagoda was the most symbolic and characteristic artificial landscape in China. His preference for pagoda featured in his campus planning. Although there was a hot debate over whether it was appropriate to built a pagoda in a garden, Murphy's design plan was finally adopted.

博雅塔
Boya Pagoda

Treasures of Yan Yuan
燕园珍藏

Chapter One: Historical Memories
第一章　历史的记忆

博雅塔与未名湖
Boya Pagoda and Weiming Lake

1.2.6 南北阁

　　南北阁的造型、体量、色彩完全一样，所以又称姐妹阁。两座阁楼与俄文楼一起构成了一个品字形的独立单元。

　　俄文楼当时被称为"课室楼"，是学生上课的地方。南北阁分别叫甘德阁和麦风阁，北边的麦风阁为音乐教室和男、女学生活动室，南边的甘德阁当时作为女部的办公楼使用。

　　北阁建成后，为纪念燕大首任女部主任麦美德女士（Mrs. Miner）被命名为"麦风阁"（Miner Hall）。南阁是麦美德博士的办公楼，1928年由甘伯尔夫人（Mrs. Gamble）捐款建造，因此命名为"甘德阁"（Gamble Hall）。麦美德博士是原华北协和女子大学的校长，华北协和女子大学并入燕京大学以后，便自动成为燕大的女部，麦美德就成为燕大首任女部主任。麦博士在任只有三年，但是为燕大做出了历史性的贡献。

南北阁
South Pavilion and North Pavilion

1.2.6 South Pavilion and North Pavilion

These two pavilions have exactly the same appearance, size and color, therefore they are also named Sister Pavilions. They as well as the Sage Hall forms an independent unit with a layout just like the shape of Chinese character "品".

The Sage Hall where students took classes was called "the Class Building" in early days. The North Pavilion was originally called "Miner Hall", serving as the music room and the activity room. And the South Pavilion was originally called "Gamble Hall", serving as the office building of women students.

After the North Pavilion was constructed, it was named Miner Hall in memory of Mrs. Miner, the first director of women students, Yenching University. The South Pavilion was once the office of Dr. Miner. It was endowed by Mrs. Gamble in 1928, and therefore was named Gamble Hall. Dr. Miner was the former president of North China Union Women University. As soon as North China Union Women University was absorbed into Yenching University, Dr. Miner became the director of women students, Yenching University. She only held this post for three years, but made historical contribution to Yenching University.

1.2.7 燕南园

燕南园是北京大学的园中之园。宁静安谧的燕南园原来是燕京大学建校之始的教师宿舍：燕南园主要为外籍教员使用，燕东园主要为中国学者居住。北大迁入燕园之后，燕南园内"居"集了众多著名的学者，不论是地理位置还是学术研究，这里都成为北大的重中之重。

燕南园并不大，总共只有17幢住宅：房屋编号从50到66号，基本未作改动。这里曾经的居住者有：洪业、向达、翦伯赞、江泽涵、周培源、饶毓泰、褚圣麟、马寅初、陈岱孙、冯友兰、汤用彤、冯定、张龙翔、王力、林焘、朱光潜、沈同、芮沐、林庚、侯仁之……

燕南园
Yannanyuan

1.2.7 Yannanyuan

Yannanyuan in Peking University seems like a garden within a garden. It was the faculties' living quarters of Yenching University during its initial stage. Foreign faculties mainly used Yannanyuan, while the Chinese faculties mainly used Yandongyuan. There were lots of famous scholars gathered and lived in Yannanyuan since Peking University moved to Yan Yuan. Furthermore, it became the heart of Peking University in both academia and geography.

Actually Yannanyuan is not a big place. There are only 17 houses in the garden in total. The houses were numbered from 50 to 66, and they remain the same up to now. As the saying goes: mountains are famous for living saints but not their height; water bodies gain magic for residing dragons but not their depth. There have been many famous figures who lived here, including Hong Ye, Xiang Da, Jian Bozan, Jiang Zehan, Zhou Peiyuan, Rao Yutai, Chu Shenglin, Ma Yinchu, Chen Daisun, Feng Youlan, Tang Yongtong, Feng Ding, Zhang Longxiang, Wang Li, Lin Tao, Zhu Guangqian, Shen Tong, Rui Mu, Lin Gen, Hou Renzhi and so on.

燕南园
Yannanyuan

1.2.8 燕东园

清乾隆年间,燕东园曾作为太监营房使用,至道光初年间作废。1921 年,燕京大学动工兴建校舍,燕东园、燕南园即为燕京大学专为中外籍教师所建的住宅区。1929 年校舍大部分落成。燕大教师住宅号码纳入全校统一安排,一个住户给一个房号。按修建年代而非地点排号,临湖轩校长住宅为 1 号,以此排下去,到燕东园寓所时号码一开始就是 21 号,直至 42 号。

此后的几十年,燕东园经历了燕大、北大两个阶段,不少学界泰斗曾入住于此,在这里留下他们的人生足迹。胡适、顾颉刚、郑振铎、张东荪、陆志韦、容庚、洪业、刘廷芳、赵紫宸、许地山、赵乃抟、俞大纲、洪谦、赵以炳、张景钺、翦伯赞等,都曾在燕东园居住过。

翦伯赞故居
Jian Bozan's House

1.2.8 Yandongyuan

Yandongyuan was used as the dormitories for eunuch in the reign of Emperor Qianlong and was abandoned in the reign of Emperor Daoguang. In 1921, Yenching University started to construct the campus. Yandongyuan and Yannanyuan were built to be the living quarters for Chinese faculties and foreign faculties. It was almost finished in 1929. The numbers of the houses were considered and arranged for the whole campus. All houses were numbered sequentially according to the construction time of the houses, thus Linhuxuan (Lake House), the residence for the president was number 1 and the other houses followed one by one. The numbers of the houses in Yandongyuan started from 21 and ended at 42.

Since then, many leading scholars have lived here and left their traces, such as Hu Shih, Gu Jiegang, Zheng Zhenduo, Zhang Dongsun, Chen Zhiwei, Rong Geng, Hong Weilian, Liu Tingfang, Zhao Zichen, Xu Dishan, Zhao Naituan, Yu Dayin, Hong Qian, Zhao Yibing, Zhang Jingyue, Jian Bozan and so on.

燕东园 21 号金岳霖教授故居
No. 21 Yandongyuan, Jin Yuelin's House

1.2.9 岛亭

1929 年，燕京大学副校长鲁斯（Harry Luce）的儿子为纪念先父，在未名湖湖心岛上捐资建亭，岛亭因此得名"鲁斯亭"（Luce Pavilion）。

此亭设有地下室，这在中国传统建筑中是不会出现的，也正因为此，它曾作为抗日杀奸团燕京小组的会址，也曾作为民主运动的秘密接头点，为进步人士提供庇护。

2013 至 2015 年间，时任北大校长王恩哥曾经常利用周四下午的时间在此邀请部分教授茶叙，商议校内教学科研事务。

鲁斯亭茶会
Faculty Afternoon Tea in the Luce Pavilion

1.2.9 Pavilion on the Islet

In memory of Henry W. Luce, the vice president of Yenching University, his son donated to build the pavilion. Thus it was named Luce Pavilion.

The pavilion was built with a basement, which definitely would not appear in Chinese traditional architectures. It was a place where the Yenching University branch of Anti-Japanese Group held their meetings. It was also a secret meeting spot for democracy movement activists and served as a safe haven for the progressive minded members of the campus.

From 2013 to 2015, Wang Enge, the President of Peking University at that time, usually hosted the Faculty Afternoon Tea on Thursday in Luce Pavilion to discuss university affairs.

岛亭
Pavilion on the Islet

1.2.10 钟亭

未名湖西南侧山顶上的钟亭内悬挂着清代宫廷内的大钟，钟身绘有龙纹、海浪及八卦图样，并有满汉文字刻写的"大清国丙申年捌月制"（1889年）。北洋水师接受慈禧检阅时，这口大钟曾作报时用。1900年它险被八国联军劫掠，后逃过战火，流落民间。1929年被燕京大学购得，成为燕大校钟，悬于湖畔山坡，同年9月正式落户在新建的玲珑雅致的圆顶攒尖钟亭内。

燕京大学行政执行委员会决议的撞钟法："每半小时撞钟一次，自十二时半起撞钟一下，一时撞两下，一时半撞三下，……四时撞八下，到四时半复撞一下。如是每四小时循环一次，每日早六时至晚十一时为撞钟时间。"

1945年日寇战败，司徒雷登在这里和工友们敲响铜钟，宣布燕大复校。

钟亭
Bell Pavilion

1.2.10 Bell Pavilion

Inside the pavilion which is located on the hill west of Weiming Lake, there is the giant bell from the royal court of Qing Dynasty. Decorated with patterns of dragon, sea wave, and the Eight Diagrams, the bell was inscribed with both Chinese and Manchu scripts: Made in the eighth month of Bing Shen year (1899 A.D.) in Great Qing Dynasty. The bell was used to tell the time when the Beiyang Fleet was being inspected by Empress Dowager Cixi. It survived the plunder of the Eight-Nation Alliance. Yenching University purchased the bell in 1929, thus it became the university bell hanging over on the hill near Weiming Lake. Then in September 1929, it was placed in the pavilion with small and exquisite round pyramid roof, which was newly built.

The schedule to ring the bell passed by administrative executive committee of Yenching University required to ring the bell every half an hour. It is also required to ring the bell "once at 12:30 am, twice at 1:00 pm, three times at 1:30 pm, …eight times at 4:00 pm and to ring it once again at 4:30 pm. It takes 4 hours as a circle, and only rings from 6:00 am to 11:00 pm."

When Japan was defeated in 1945, President John Leighton Stuart rang the bell with his co-workers to declare the re-opening of Yenching University.

1.3 圆明园遗珍
1.3 Relics of the Old Summer Palace

1.3.1 华表

华表据传源于古时的"诽谤木",供臣民书写意见,品评是非之用。后主要立于宫殿、陵墓之前,成为皇家才有权利使用的标志物。

现在北大西门内的两座华表原置于圆明园安佑宫琉璃牌坊前,搬运时两对弄混。因此,现在看到的华表一粗一细,并非一对。另两座立在中国国家图书馆古籍馆前。

华表(摄影/何晋)
Ornamental Columns(Photography by He Jin)

1.3.1 Ornamental Columns

The Ornamental Columns originated from "Feibang Mu" (Criticisms Wood) in the past, which was used by the people to write comments and evaluations. Afterwards, it was placed in front of palaces and mausoleums, and only the imperial family could use it. Thus it had become the symbol of the royal family.

The two ornamental columns that stand in front of the Administrative Building came from the An You Palace of the Old Summer Palace. They were mixed up with another two columns during the transportation. Thus one of the ornamental columns was larger than the other one, and they were not made a pair. The rest of these two pairs are now in front of the Ancient Books Library of the National Library of China.

华表
Ornamental Columns

1.3.2 石麒麟和丹墀

石麒麟蹲坐于束腰须弥座上。它们是圆明园安佑宫的遗物，现置于办公楼前。

圆明园被毁之后，所幸这对石麒麟没有遭到破坏。此后很久，石麒麟一直留在圆明园内。到清末时，被文物盗卖者从中盗出，准备高价出卖。当时的朗润园园主载涛知道后，便出高价买到这对石麒麟和安佑宫前云龙纹丹墀，后来载涛把朗润园卖给燕大作为新校址，石麒麟和丹墀也归燕大所有。

石麒麟
Stone Kylin

1.3.2 Stone Kylin and Vermilion Palace Steps

The kylins squatted on the sumeru base with a waist. They are the relic of An You Palace of Old Summer Palace, and are placed in front of the Administrative Building now. Kylins, the decoration that can only be used by the royal family in the past show the importance of the Administrative Building among all the buildings in Yan Yuan.

Luckily the kylins weren't damaged after the destruction of Old Summer Palace. Since then, the kylins remained in Old Summer Palace until they were stolen and were about to be sold at a high price in the late Qing Dynasty. Zaitao, the owner of Langrunyuan then, got the information and bought the kylins and the stone Vermilion Palace Steps at a high price. Later, as Zaitao sold Langrunyuan to Yenching University to be the new university campus, the Stone Kylins and the Vermilion Palace Steps, which once belonged to the An You Palace, were also given to Yenching University.

丹墀
The Vermilion Palace Steps

Treasures of Yan Yuan
燕园珍藏

1.3.3 翻尾石鱼

　　翻尾石鱼为圆明园中长春园"谐奇趣"中遗物，造型奇特，身雕鳞状纹、张口朝天，现成为未名湖水中最为灵动的点缀。1860年圆明园被焚毁后，翻尾石鱼也被变卖，后来被朗润园的主人载涛买下运到朗润园并在园中放置多年。燕京大学1930届学生毕业时，将此石鱼买来送给母校，安置在未名湖畔。

翻尾石鱼
Roll-Tailed Stone Fish

1.3.3 Roll-Tailed Stone Fish

Roll-Tailed Stone Fish, a relic of "Xie Qi Qu Garden" in the Old Summer Palace, is in a unique shape with squamous body and an upturned mouth. It is the most vivid decoration in Weiming Lake. When the Old Summer Palace was destroyed in 1860, the stone fish was sold. Afterwards, it was bought by Zaitao, the owner of Langrunyuan. And it was placed in the garden for years. Later it was purchased by graduates of Yenching University in 1930 as a gift to the university and placed in Weiming Lake.

1.3.4 四扇屏

现未名湖北畔的四扇屏上有乾隆题写的两副对联,是圆明园四十景之一"夹镜鸣琴"遗物。虽然经过几百年的风吹雨打,其上字迹仍然清晰可辨。第一至第四扇石屏上所题依次为:

画舫平临苹岸阔
飞楼俯映柳荫多
夹镜光澄风四面
垂虹影界水中央

1.3.4 Four Stone Tablets

With two pairs of couplets written by Emperor Qianlong, the four tablets were relics of "Jia Jing Ming Qin", one of the "Forty scenes of Old Summer Palace". Although they have been exposed to wind and rain for several hundreds of years, the writings on these stones are still clear and distinguishable. On these four stone tablets, words are inscribed as follow:

>   *The pleasure boat lies by the side of the lake against the wide bank.*
>   *Buildings with upturned eaves and weeping willows are reflected in water.*
>   *The lake is bright like a mirror with breezes coming from all directions.*
>   *The rainbow sheds its shadow as if falling into the water.*

Chapter One: Historical Memories
第一章 历史的记忆

四扇屏
Four Stone Tablets

1.3.5 花池

　　花池也是圆明园安佑宫遗物，现在临湖轩南侧。花池作须弥座造型，须弥座源于印度古代传说中世界的中心——须弥山，随着佛教的传入，象征着神圣尊贵、敦实稳重的须弥座形象被广泛用于皇家贵族的建筑中。在燕园中，有须弥座的除此之外，还有石狮、石麒麟、华表、办公楼、博雅塔和五贡桌等。

花池
Hua Chi

1.3.5 Hua Chi

Located on the south side of Lake House, Hua Chi (The Flora Basin) is a relic of the An You Palace of the Old Summer Palace. It is in the shape of Sumeru, which originated from Mount Sumeru, the center of the world in ancient legends of India.

Along with the introduction and development of Buddhism in China, the pattern of Sumeru, which symbolizes the holiness and dignity, was widely adopted on royal architecture. Besides the Flora Basin, one could also find the pattern of Sumeru on Stone Lions, Stone Kylins, Ornamental Columns, Administrative Building, Boya Pagoda and Five Articles of Tributes in Stone Sculpture.

1.3.6 五孔溪桥

从德、才、均、备斋通往未名湖湖心岛，需要经过这座唯一的石桥。这座石桥原来是圆明园西洋楼方外观门前之五孔溪桥，圆明园被烧毁后，石桥也被人拆走，后来被燕京大学购回得以保存，但桥面原来西式石栏杆已不存在。

Chapter One: Historical Memories
第一章 历史的记忆

1.3.6 Five-Arch Creek Bridge

Five-Arch Creek Bridge is the only access from De Zhai, Cai Zhai, Jun Zhai and Bei Zhai to the Center Islet in the Weiming Lake. The bridge was the Five-Arch Creek Bridge in front of Fang Wai Guan of Xiyanglou in the Old Summer Palace. It was dismantled and taken away after the Old Summer Palace was destroyed. Later Yenching University purchased and preserved it. However, the western style stone handrail had been lost.

五孔溪桥
Five-Arch Creek Bridge

1.3.7 梅石碑

此碑原置于圆明园长春园茜园内，碑的阳面正中刻有一株苍枝老干的苔梅，旁边刻奇石"青莲朵"，碑阴镌刻乾隆皇帝御笔题诗一首。

南宋高宗赵构德寿宫内，有梅一株，梅旁有名为"芙蓉石"，又称"德寿石"的怪石一方。明代时，梅花枯萎，画家孙杕在"芙蓉石"旁立一块石碑，并刻画一株梅花于其上。后画家蓝瑛将"芙蓉石"也刻画于碑上，即为梅石碑。

乾隆南巡，在游览德寿宫遗迹时发现了"芙蓉石"和已断残倒地的梅石碑，深表喜爱并赋诗一首："傍峰不见旧梅英，石道无情迹怆情。此日荒凉德寿月，只余碑版照蓝瑛。"

后来，乾隆又照着原碑摹刻了两块，并将其所作诗文也刻于其上，一块立于杭州德寿宫遗址处，一块安放在圆明园内"芙蓉石"旁，以重现当年之景。

梅石碑
Meishi Tablet

1.3.7 Meishi Tablet (The Tablet Carved with Plums and Stone)

The tablet was originally placed in Qian Yuan of Old Summer Palace. There is an old plum tree with grey and aged branches in the middle of its sun-facing side. And the fancy rock named "Qing Lian Duo" stands by the side of the tree. There is a poem written by Emperor Qianlong on its back side.

There was a plum tree in Southern Song Emperor Gaozong's Deshou Palace. At the side, the tree stood a unique rock called "Furong Stone" ("Peony Stone"), also known as "Deshou Stone". The plum tree perished during the Ming Dynasty. Sun Di, a painter, placed a tablet with a carved plum tree next to the Furong Stone. Later Lan Ying, another painter, carved the Furong Stone on the tablet, thus forming the Meishi Tablet.

Emperor Qianlong found "Furong Stone" and the already broken Meishi Tablet on the site of Deshou Palace during his journey to the south. He was keen on them and wrote a poem:

Gone are the blooming plum trees near the peak,
The site makes people sorrowful with the cold and ruthless stones.
Bleak stone has exhausted its charm.
Only the tablet recalls the old days and the old people.

Later, Emperor Qianlong copied the original tablet to carve another two, and put his literal works on the stones to revisit those heady days. One was placed on the site of Deshou Palace in Hangzhou, while the other was placed next to the "Furong Stone" in Old Summer Palace.

1.4 建筑小品

1.4 Architectural Oddments

英法联军1860年洗劫焚烧圆明园，民国时期，军阀、官僚、政客又大肆劫掠和强购园内文物，致使许多圆明园文物流落民间。燕京大学因为"近水楼台"购买和收藏了一些圆明园的遗物，如北大西门内原圆明园安佑宫前的华表、石麒麟、龙云纹丹墀，圆明园谐奇趣楼南大型海棠式喷水池中的翻尾石鱼，圆明园四十景之一"夹镜鸣琴"中的乾隆四扇屏等。除了明清旧园和圆明园的这些文物，还有一些建筑小品，也已经成为北大校园中标志性的建筑物。

Chapter One: Historical Memories
第一章 历史的记忆

In 1860, the British and French allied forces looted and burned the Old Summer Palace. During the period of the Republic of China, warlords, bureaucrats and politicians wantonly looted and bought cultural relics in the park, which caused many artifacts from Old Summer Palace became private collections. Because of its convenient location, Yenching University purchased many artifacts from the Old Summer Palace, such as ornamental columns formerly in front of An You Palace, Stone Kylins, Vermilion Palace Steps with dragon and Cloud Relief, Roll-Tailed Stone Fish from the large fountain pool of Xie Qi Qu, and Four Stone Tablets from "Jia Jing Ming Qin", one of the Forty Scenic Spots of Old Summer Palace. Besides the relics from former gardens in Ming and Qing Dynasties and from the Old Summer Palace, there are a number of architectural oddments, which have become landmarks of Peking University.

1.4.1 日晷

　　现立于赛克勒考古与艺术博物馆前的日晷由汉白玉制成。高近三米,分大底座、碑身和日晷三部分。碑身从北开始按顺时针方向刻着篆字碑文。碑文分别为:"近取诸物""远取诸身""仰以观于天文""俯以察于地理"。碑身以上为日晷,由底座、晷盘及晷针组成。日晷利用日影测算时间,虽是计时工具,但在古代为皇家所专有。

　　此文物原置于北沙滩老北大物理系门前。北大物理学院新园区落成后,一些师生希望将其搬回学院。2018年10月,院友王恩哥向学院捐赠一复制日晷,现立于物理学院院内。

日晷
Sundial

1.4.1 Sundial

A Sundial is now located in front of the Arthur M. Sackler Museum of Art and Archaeology. Made by white marbles, it is 3 meters high and consists of a big base, the body and the sundial. The four-faced body has carvings of proverbs from Yi Jing and Zhou Yi on each side clockwise from north. The sundial itself consists of base, plate and needle. The sundials use shadows of the sun to calculate time. Though it is just a timekeeping device, it was exclusive for royal uses in the past.

This Sundial once stood in front of the Department of Physics, the former Peking University at Shatan. In 2018, Enge Wang donated to the School of Physics a sundial replica, which stands now in the school's courtyard.

日晷
Sundial

1.4.2 杭爱碑

杭爱（？—1683），满洲镶白旗人，康熙时的封疆大吏，历任吏部郎中、山西布政使、陕西巡抚和四川巡抚。清政府平定"三藩之乱"期间，负责督办军饷。任四川巡抚期间，平定叛乱，整修都江堰，都江堰现在还有其功德铭。卒于康熙二十二年，皇帝赐谥号"勤襄"。

石碑原来立于六院和俄文楼之间的土山上，燕京大学大规模兴建新校址时移于静园草坪东北角和西北角竹丛中。石碑立于清康熙二十四年，由碑首、碑身、碑座三部分构成。碑身上有用满、汉两种文字书写的碑文。

杭爱碑
Hang Ai Tablet

1.4.2 Hang Ai Tablet

Hang Ai (? – 1683), belonged to the Bordered White Banner. He was a high officer during the reign of Emperor Kangxi. He successively held the posts of Langzhong of Ministry of Personnel, Shanxi provincial commissioner, the governor of Shaanxi, and the governor of Sichuan. During the suppression of the "Revolt of the Three Feudatories" by the Qing government, he supervised and handled the affairs of military expenditures. Later on his term in Sichuan, he crushed rebellions, and restored Dujiang Weir. Even now there is an inscription for the merits and virtues of Hang Ai at Dujiang Weir. He died in the 22nd year of Kangxi (1682). The emperor gave him a posthumous title called "Qin Xiang", meaning his diligence and capability on government affairs.

The stone originally stood at the earth mound between the Sixth Courtyard and the Sage Hall. During the large-scale construction of the new campus of Yenching University, it was moved to the bamboo forest at the northeast corner of Jingyuan lawn. Established in the twenty-fourth year of Kangxi (1684), the monument is composed of three parts. The memorial inscription is written in Manchu script and Chinese characters.

杭爱碑
Hang Ai Tablet

1.4.3 葛利普教授之墓

北大西门南侧，有一个墓碑格外显眼，在此长眠的主人叫葛利普（Amadeus William Grabau，1870—1946）。

葛利普先生曾任美国哥伦比亚大学教授，经丁文江先生推荐，1920年被北大聘为地质学教授。他来到北大时已年满50岁，但以极大的热情投入到培养中国年轻地质工作者的工作中。

1946年3月20日，葛利普在北京病逝。他视中国为第二故乡，生前要求加入中国国籍，但由于抗战爆发未能如愿。按照他的生前愿望，北大教授会一致通过决议，将葛利普教授骨灰安葬于北大地质馆前（原沙滩嵩公府夹道，现沙滩北街15号）。1982年7月，北大将葛利普墓迁至燕园主校区，坐落在西校门内苍松翠柏之中。墓碑是山岳的造型，微微向上耸立，坚韧而凝重。墓碑上葛利普教授的侧面头像，让人得以遥想先生当年严谨的治学态度和坚毅的个人品格。

葛利普教授之墓
Tomb of Professor Grabau

1.4.3 Tomb of Professor Grabau

A tombstone stands particularly conspicuous at the south side of the west gate of Peking University. The person who peacefully rests here is Professor Amadeus William Grabau (1870 – 1946).

Mr. Grabau once was a professor at the Columbia University. Recommended by Mr. Ding Wenjiang, he was appointed as a professor of Geology by Peking University in 1920. When he came to Peking University, he was already 50 years old, and devoted with great enthusiasm to the training of young geologists in China.

Grabau died in Beijing on March 20th, 1946. He regarded China as the second hometown and asked to join Chinese nationality before his death. However, he failed to do so because of the outbreak of the Anti-Japanese War. According to his wishes, professors of Peking University unanimously adopted a resolution to bury Professor Grabau's ashes in front of the Geology Hall of Peking University (No. 15 of the original Songgong Fu walk, now Shatan North Street) just as his wish. In July 1982, Peking University moved Professor Grabau's tomb to Yan Yuan. The tomb now locates inside the west gate and in the green pines and verdant cypresses. The tombstone has the shape of a mountain, slightly upward, tough and dignified. The tombstone was carved with Professor Grabau's profile, which recalls his rigorousness as a scholar and his resolution as a gentleman.

1.4.4 斯诺之墓

"他的一部分占了圆明园的旧址,保持了原来的景色,包括校园中心那个花园一般的可爱的小湖。"——这是埃德加·斯诺(Edgar Snow,1905—1972),后来回忆当年的燕园景色时在书中写到的一段话。

斯诺说到的那个小湖,即是今天北大校园内秀雅多姿的未名湖。未名湖的四周,绿树掩映,景色宜人。在它的南面正对着慈济寺庙门的方向,拾阶而上就可以看到埃德加·斯诺的墓园。

墓园占地面积不大,于小山之上辟出宁静的一隅。在其中央安放着一块洁白的汉白玉墓碑,上面书写着:"中国人民的美国朋友埃德加·斯诺之墓 叶剑英 一九七七年十二月二十三日"的字样。墓园依山而建,时常会有人慕名而来,瞻仰悼念。时光荏苒,每当你走近它仍会感觉到那种沉静中透出来的安详,静谧中孕育着的生机。

斯诺之墓
Tomb of Edgar Snow

1.4.4 Tomb of Edgar Snow

"Part of it occupies the former site of Old Summer Palace, including the lovely small lake in the center of the garden-like campus." These were the words written by Edgar Snow (1905 – 1972) in his book when he recalled the scenery of Yan Yuan.

The small lake Snow mentioned is the Weiming Lake in the campus of Peking University. Surrounded by trees, Weiming Lake has pleasant scenery. At the south side of the lake and facing the direction of Ci Ji Temple, one could climb the stairs and see the tomb of Snow.

The tomb covers a small area and gives a quiet corner over the hills. In the center there is a piece of white marble tombstone with inscription: "IN MEMORY OF EDGAR SNOW. AN AMERICAN FRIEND OF THE CHINESE PEOPLE 1905 – 1972".

1.4.5 赖朴吾、夏仁德之墓

漫步于未名湖畔，有时在不经意间会发现一处别致的墓碑，这就是曾在燕京大学任教的赖朴吾和夏仁德两位先生的墓园。墓园坐落在临湖轩所在的小山的脚下，迎面朝向未名湖，依傍山体，临水而立。

赖朴吾教授（Ernest Ralph Lapwood, 1909—1984）出生于英国的伯明翰，是著名的数学家和地球物理学家，他毕业于剑桥大学，主修数学，获得硕士学位。后来来到了中国，他将毕生的精力奉献给了中国的教育事业。

与赖朴吾教授的名字共同刻于碑上的是夏仁德教授。夏仁德（Randolph Clothier Sailer，1898—1981）出生在美国宾西法尼亚州的费城，1923 年取得美国哥伦比亚大学博士学位。从 1923 年到 1950 年，除燕京大学被日本占领的时期，夏仁德一直在燕京大学心理系任教。虽然他的遗骨没有葬在这里，但在燕园中留下了他深深的印记。所以为了使后来人永远将他铭记于心，学校也将他的名字刻在了墓碑上。

赖朴吾、夏仁德之墓
Tomb of Lapwood and Sailer

1.4.5 Tomb of Lapwood and Sailer

When people wander along the Weiming Lake, sometimes they may inadvertently discover a unique tombstone, which signs the tomb of Mr. Lapwood and Mr. Sailer who used to teach in Yenching University. The tomb locates at the foot of the hill where stands the Lake House. Facing the lake, the tomb lies along the hill and near the water.

Born in Birmingham, England, Professor Ernest Ralph Lapwood was a famous mathematician and geophysicist. He graduated from the University of Cambridge, majoring in mathematics, and got a master's degree. Later, he came to China and devoted his whole life to the cause of education in China.

Along with Professor Ernest Ralph Lapwood inscribed on the tombstone is the name of Professor Randolph Clothier Sailer. He was born in Philadelphia, Pennsylvania, in 1923 and received a Ph.D. from Columbia University. From 1923 to 1950 (except the period when Yenching University was occupied by Japanese), Professor Randolph Clothier Sailer taught in the Department of Psychology all the time. Although his remains was not buried here, he has left deep impression in Yan Yuan. Therefore, his name was inscribed on the tombstone as well.

Chapter Two
Knowledge Inheritance

第二章
知识的传承

燕园不仅是一个地理意义上的存在，对于北大人而言，更是一种集体意义上共同气质与追求的精神家园。作为中国第一所国立综合性大学，北京大学在知识的传承与创新、民族的解放和振兴、国家的建设和发展、社会的文明和进步中做出了不可替代的贡献，在中国走向伟大复兴的进程中起到了重要的作用。在第二章，我们从历史的丰富积淀中择其精要，选取一些代表性的故事呈现给读者，其中既涵盖了人文精神领域北大风骨气质的典型体现，又囊括了数学、物理、化学、地学、生命、医学等基础科学的成果代表。贯穿其中的，都是燕园土地上不同领域的学者们对于精神、知识和创新的探索与贡献。以"知识的传承"为题，抚今追昔，意在如此。

Chapter Two: Knowledge Inheritance
第二章 知识的传承

Peking University campus, namely Yan Yuan, is not only a geographical existence, but also a spiritual home for the people who share collective temperament and pursuit. As China's first national comprehensive university, Peking University has made irreplaceable contributions in the inheritance and innovation of knowledge, the rejuvenation and liberation of the nation, the construction and development of the country, and the civilization and progress of the society. Above all, Peking University acted as a pioneer in the process of China's modernization. In this chapter, we select some representative stories out of numerous historical accumulation for the readers. They include not only some representative fruits in the fields of arts and humanities, but also scientific achievements in mathematics, physics, chemistry, earth science, life science, medicine and so forth. Through them, we could witness the exploration and contribution of Peking University scholars in different fields, which echoes the theme of "Knowledge Inheritance".

蔡元培校长
President Cai Yuanpei

2.1 校风传承
2.1 Inheritance of School Spirits

2.1.1 《论北京大学校不可停办说帖》

严复所写的《论北京大学校不可停办说帖》（现藏北大档案馆）是北大历史上的一份重要文稿。1912年7月，当时的政府以水平不高、经费困难等理由欲停办北京大学，严复写下此帖，不仅有力驳斥了停办北大的各种借口，且进一步指出，大学的意义，不仅在于培养专门人才，更重要的是"保存一切高尚之学术，以崇国家之文化"。同年，严复在《分科大学改良办法说帖》中强调北大要成为"一国学业之中心点"，"理宜兼收并蓄，广纳众流，以成其大"。

严复是清末著名的翻译家和思想家，1902年受聘为京师大学堂译书局总办，1912年2月任京师大学堂总监督，同年5月，京师大学堂改称北京大学，严复任首任校长兼文科学长，1912年10月被迫辞去北大校长职务。

2.1.1 *On the School of Peking University Cannot be Closed*

The memorandum *On the School of Peking University Cannot be Closed* Yan Fu wrote in 1912 (the first year of the Republic of China) (from the Archives of Peking University) is an important document in the history of Peking University. In July 1912, the government intended to shut down Peking University with the excuses of low education quality and financial difficulties. The post written by Yan Fu refutes the various excuses for the closure of Peking University. It further pointed out that the significance of the university, is not only to cultivate specialized talents, but more importantly, is to "preserve all refined learning to uphold the culture of the nation." In the same year, Yan Fu wrote a memorandum on *Ways to Improve Division of the University into Branches*, in which he emphasized that Peking University would become "the national center of academics", "establishing its greatness by being eclectic and broad ranging".

Yan Fu was hired in the Imperial University Publishing House general office in 1902. In February 1912, he became the School Superintendent of Imperial University of Peking, which was renamed Peking University in the same year, where Yan Fu served as the first president and director of liberal arts. In October 1912, due to Yan Fu's struggle for the development of the university, he offended the authorities and was forced to resign as president of Peking University.

《论北京大学校不可停办说帖》
On the School of Peking University Cannot be Closed

2.1.2 校长简任状函

这是1917年教育部转送蔡元培的北京大学校长简任状函（现藏于北大档案馆，其任命状现藏于蔡元培上海故居纪念馆）。1916年12月，受时任大总统黎元洪任命，蔡元培成为北大校长。从1917年到任至1927年的十年间，蔡元培深刻地影响和改变了北大，他自己也因此享有北大"永远的校长"之名。蔡元培首先明确大学的性质是"研究高深学问者也"，而非"官僚养成所"。在学校管理上，他主张教授治校，民主管理。蔡元培倡导"思想自由，兼容并包"，并依此原则延揽人才，"囊括大典，网罗众家"，一时之间，北大汇聚了各种思想的代表性人物，如陈独秀、李大钊、胡适、梁漱溟、鲁迅等，极大地活跃了从校园到社会的思想文化氛围。杜威评价说："拿世界各国的大学校长来比较，牛津、剑桥、巴黎、柏林、哈佛等大学校长中，在某些学科有卓越贡献的不乏其人；但是，以一个校长身份，能领导一所大学，对一个民族、一个时代起到引领作用的，除蔡元培外，恐怕找不出第二个人。"

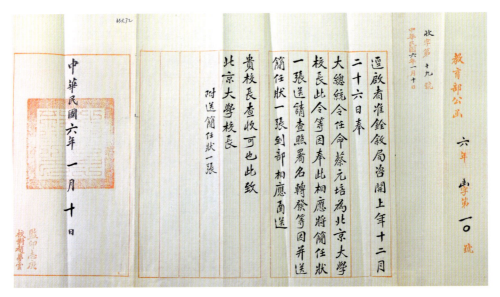

校长简任状函
Appointment Letter of President Cai Yuanpei

2.1.2 Appointment Letter of President Cai Yuanpei

This is the appointment letter from Ministry of Education to Cai Yuanpei (from the Archives of Peking University, the original letter is now in the possession of the Cai Yuanpei Memorial in Shanghai).

Cai Yuanpei was appointed president of Peking University in December 1916. In the following ten years since then, Cai Yuanpei profoundly influenced and changed Peking University, and achieved the title of the "Forever President of Peking University". First, Cai made it clear that the nature of the university was "the study of advanced learning" rather than a "bureaucracy". He advocated that professors should play a crucial role in university management. Cai encouraged the principle of "free to think, open to absorb anything" and furthermore recruited talents according to these principles. "Bringing together collections of classical writings and all schools of thought under one umbrella", Peking University brought together various profound thinkers, such as Chen Duxiu, Li Dazhao, Hu Shih, Liang Shuming, Lu Xun and others, whom all greatly stimulated the ideological and cultural atmosphere from the campus to the society. Dewey said, "comparing university presidents from all over the world, such as the universities of Oxford, Cambridge, Paris, Berlin, Harvard and so on, there is no lack of people who made outstanding contributions in certain subjects, but in the regard that a university leader could guide a higher education institution to make a turning effect on one nation and one era, I cannot find a person second to President Cai Yuanpei."

2.1.3 北大之精神

"北大之精神"是蒋梦麟1923年12月17日以代理校长身份在北大纪念会上的演讲。蒋梦麟认为，北大之所以能够在危险的环境中巍然独存，在于其拥有大度包容和思想自由的精神。但由此精神也产生两种缺点：能容则择宽而纪律弛，思想自由则个性发达而群治弛。因此他呼吁北大应该整饬纪律，发展群治。

蒋梦麟是民国时期著名的教育家，1908年赴美国读书，1917年获得哥伦比亚大学博士学位。1919—1926年任北大教授，并数次代理校长。1930年正式出任北大校长，一直到1945年。担任校长期间，提出"教授治学，学生求学，职员治事，校长治校"的方针。

蒋梦麟：北大之精神

本校屡经风潮，至今犹能巍然独存，决非偶然之事。这几年来，我们全校一致的奋斗，已不止一次了。当在奋斗的时候，危险万状，本校命运有朝不保夕之势；到底每一次的奋斗，本校终得胜利，这是什么缘故呢？

第一，本校具有大度包容的精神。俗语说："宰相肚里好撑船"，这是说一个人能容，才可以做总握万机的宰相。若是气度狭窄，容不了各种的人，就不配当这样的大位。凡历史上雍容有度的名相，无论经过何种的大难，未有不能巍然独存的。千百年后，反对者、讥议者的遗骨已经过变成灰土；而名相的声誉犹照耀千古，"时愈久而名愈彰"。

个人如此，机关亦如此。凡一个机关只能容一派的人，或一种的思想的，到底必因环境变迁而死。即使苟延残喘，窄而陋的学术机关，于社会决无甚贡献。虽不死，犹和死了的一般。

本校自蔡先生长校以来，七八年间这个"容"字，已在本校的肥土之中，

左起：蒋梦麟、蔡元培、胡适、李大钊等卧佛寺合影
From Left: Jiang Menglin, Cai Yuanpei, Hu Shih, Li Dazhao

根深蒂固了。故本校内各派别均能互相容受。平时于讲堂之内，会议席之上，作剧烈的辩驳和争论，一到患难的时候，便共力合作。这是已屡经试验的了。

但容量无止境，我们当继续不断地向"容"字一方面努力。"宰相肚里好撑船"。本校"肚里"要好驶飞艇才好！

第二，本校具有思想自由的精神。人类有一个弱点，就是对于思想自由，发露他是一个小胆鬼。思想些许越出本身日常习惯范围以外，一般人们恐慌起来，好像不会撑船的人，越了平时习惯的途径一样。但这个思想上的小胆鬼，被本校渐渐儿的压服了。本校是不怕越出人类本身日常习惯范围以外去运用思想的。虽然我们自己有时还觉得有许多束缚，而一般社会已送了我们一个洪水猛兽的徽号。

本校里面，各种思想能自由发展，不受一种统一思想所压迫，故各种思想虽平时互相歧异，到了有某种思想受外部压迫时，就共同来御外侮。引外力以排除异己，是本校所不为的。故本校虽处恶劣政治环境之内，尚能安然无恙。

我们有了这两种的特点，因此而产生两种缺点。能容则择宽而纪律弛；思想自由，则个性发达而群治弛。故此后本校当于相当范围以内，整饬纪律，发展群治，以补本校之不足。

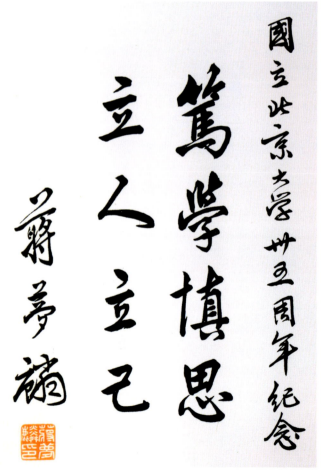

蒋梦麟手迹
Jiang Menglin's Original Handwriting

2.1.3 The Spirit of Peking University

"The Spirit of Peking University" is Jiang Menglin's speech as an acting president of Peking University on December 17, 1923. Jiang Menglin believed that Peking University was in a dangerous environment and standed alone, because its spirit encouraged tolerance and freedom of thought. However, there were two kinds of shortcomings in this spirit: tolerance was wide-ranging selections, but it loosened discipline, while freedom of thought developed individualism but disseminated the collectivism. Henceforth he called out that Peking University should strengthen discipline and develop as a whole group.

Jiang Menglin was a famous educator in the Republic of China. He went to the United States to study in 1908 and received his doctorate from Columbia University in 1917. From 1919 – 1926 he served as professor at Peking University and served as an acting president several times. Between 1930 to 1945 he served as president of Peking University. During the period of his presidency, he advocated the policy of "professors focus on studies, academia seeks learning, staff manages daily affairs and the president leads the school."

2.1.4《北京大学五十周年纪念特刊》

下图中的文稿是胡适 1948 年在纪念北大创办五十周年时的讲话稿（现藏北大档案馆）。讲话能够反映出胡适对于大学的理解，一是以学术为中心，尤其提到蔡元培与蒋梦麟的贡献，两位先生相继主持北大三十年，把北大营造成为一个持续发展的学术中心。二是延揽人才的重要性，其中特别提到蒋梦麟利用中华教育文化基金董事会的支持，"向全国去挑选教授与研究的人才"。1926 年胡适在致蔡元培的信中曾经感慨："今天忍不住，又写此信与先生，现在学校的好教员都要走了。"三是校长的魄力和担当，"辞退旧人，我去做；选聘新人，你们去做。"

胡适 1917 年学成回国后便任教北大，是新文化运动的重要领袖之一。在北大先后工作十八年，担任北大教授（1917—1925）、文学院长（1930—1937）、北大校长（1946—1948），为北大的发展做出了重要贡献。

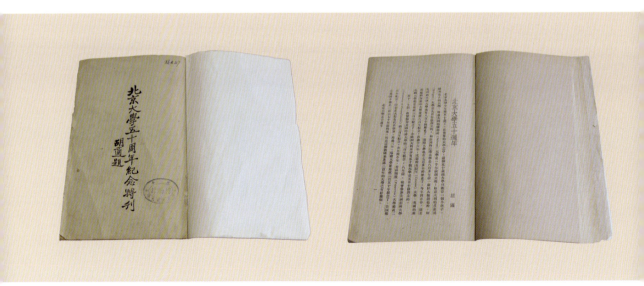

《北京大学五十周年纪念特刊》
50th Anniversary Commemorative Edition of Peking University

2.1.4 50th Anniversary Commemorative Edition of Peking University

The document below is a speech made by Hu Shih in 1948 to commemorate the 50th anniversary of Peking University (from the Archives of Peking University). The speech reflects Hu Shih's understanding towards the university. One point is to take academics as its focus, especially emphasizing the contributions made by Presidents Cai Yuanpei and Jiang Menglin. The two gentlemen presided over the University for thirty years, and turned Peking University into an academic center. The second point is the importance of recruiting talents, with particular reference to Jiang Menglin using the support from the board of directors of the foundation for Chinese Education and Culture "selecting professors and researchers from the entire nation." In 1926, Hu Shih expressed his sorrow in a letter to Cai Yuanpei, "Today I could not bear but to write this letter, now that the best teachers have to go…" The third point is the president's courage and play: "dismissing the elder generation is my job, hiring the future generation is your job."

After returning to his motherland in 1917, Hu Shih joined the faculty in Peking University, until his departure in December 1948. During those eighteen years, he served as a professor at Peking University (1917 – 1925), Dean of Humanities (1930 – 1937), and President of the University (1946 – 1948). He made enormous contributions to the development of Peking University.

北京大学五十周年纪念特刊
50th Anniversary Commemorative Edition of Peking University

2.1.5 《新青年》

《新青年》是中国文化史上一本具有里程碑意义的杂志。初名《青年杂志》,由陈独秀 1915 年创刊于上海,1916 年 9 月出版第二卷第一号时改名为《新青年》。陈独秀 1916 年受聘为北大文科学长之后,《新青年》编辑部 1917 年随迁至北京,1926 年停刊。《青年杂志》创办之初,即明确主张科学与民主,要求青年秉持六种态度:自主的而非奴隶的、进步的而非保守的、进取的而非退隐的、世界的而非锁国的、实利的而非虚文的、科学的而非想象的。《新青年》宣传先进文化,反对旧文化,是现代启蒙和马克思主义传播的重要阵地。胡适的《文学改良刍议》、鲁迅的《狂人日记》、李大钊的《庶民的胜利》均发表于此,极大地影响了现代中国的政治、社会和文化。

《新青年》
The Magazine *New Youth* (French: *La Jeunesse*)

2.1.5 The Magazine *New Youth* (French: *La Jeunesse*)

The *New Youth* is a landmark magazine in the history of Chinese culture. It was founded by Chen Duxiu in 1915 in Shanghai, first named *Youth Magazine* and renamed *New Youth* in 1916. Its headquarters were moved to Beijing in January 1917 when Chen was appointed Chairman of the Chinese Literature Department of Peking University. The magazine was shut down in 1926 by the Nationalist Government.

Since its publication, the magazine was dedicated to promoting science and democracy. Chen published "A Letter to Youth" in the first issue, encouraging the youngsters to uphold six attitudes: to be independent and not enslaved, be progressive and not conservative, be in the forefront and not lagging behind, be internationalist and not isolationist, be practical and not rhetorical, be scientific and not superstitious. The magazine had an emphasis on the new vernacular literature revolution and the social revolution, against the established traditional society and confucian values. It initiated the New Culture Movement and became an important platform for the enlightenment of people and the spread of Marxism. Some landmark articles and stories like "Essay on Creating a Revolutionary New Literature" by Hu Shih, "A Madman's Diary" by Lu Xun, "Plebeian Victory" by Li Dazhao were all published on the *New Youth* magazine, which greatly influenced the politics, society and culture of modern China.

2.1.6 《新人口论》

1957年4月27日，马寅初在北大大饭厅做人口问题的报告，主要内容是控制人口数量，提高人口质量，实行计划生育。同年7月5日，马寅初的《新人口论》全文刊登在《人民日报》上。文章一经发表，便引起了激烈争论，马寅初也因此受到错误批评。然而，马寅初坚持真理，在随后出版的《我的哲学思想和经济理论》一文中，他说："我虽年近八十，明知寡不敌众，自当单枪匹马，出来迎战，直至战死为止，决不向专以力压服人不以理说服的那种批判者们投降。"

马寅初是中国最早一批在国外获得经济学博士学位的留学生之一，也是北大经济学科的奠基者之一。1916年任北大经济学教授，1919年任北大第一任教务长。1951年出任新中国首任北大校长，直至1960年在《新人口论》引起的激烈争论与批判中辞职。

马寅初与学生
President Ma Yinchu with Students

2.1.6 The Book *Discussions on New Populations*

On April 27, 1957, Ma Yinchu gave a presentation on China's population issues in the dining hall of Peking University. The main contents involve control over population growth, quality improvement and implementation of family planning. On July 5 of the same year, the full text of Ma Yinchu's *Discussions on New Populations* was published in *People's Daily*. After the article was published, it caused a heated debate and Ma Yinchu was wrongly criticized because of it. However, Ma Yinchu persisted in the truth, and later in his *My Philosophy and Economic Theory* he said, "although I am nearly eighty years old and fully aware of the possibility I could win, yet I stand alone unaccompanied, meeting the enemy in this battle towards death. I will not surrender to those who cannot persuade but simply force people into submission."

Ma Yinchu, one of the first-generation Chinese students who earned a doctorate in economics abroad, is also one of the founders of the School of Economics in Peking University. In 1916, he was a professor of Economics at Peking University and became the first provost of Peking University in 1919. Ma Yinchu became the president of Peking University in 1951 and resigned in the fierce controversy and criticism caused by *Discussions on New Populations* in 1960.

马寅初《新人口论》的部分手稿（现藏于北京大学档案所）
Part of Ma Yinchu's Handwritten Manuscript *Discussions on New Populations* (Archives of Peking University)

2.2 知识创新
2.2 Knowledge Innovation

2.2.1 《国立北京大学自然科学季刊》创刊号

1929年10月1日,《国立北京大学自然科学季刊》在北平创刊。蔡元培亲自题写刊名,经利彬任主编。该刊由国立北京大学科学季刊委员会编辑,国立北京大学出版部出版发行。

大学自然科学学报和期刊的萌芽,依赖于大学及相应理工科学系的开设和教育研究的深入发展。经过"五四"新文化运动的洗礼,人们极大地解放了思想,我国大学及科学文化教育得到快速发展,《国立北京大学自然科学季刊》为中国现代科学技术事业的传播与进步做出了重要贡献。

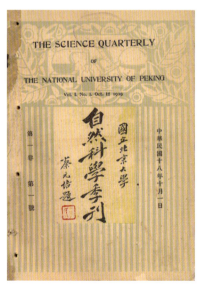

自然科学季刊
The First Issue of *The Science Quarterly*

2.2.1 First Issue of *The Science Quarterly of National University of Peking*

On October 1, 1929, the history witnessed the first issue of *The Science Quarterly of National University of Peking*, whose title was inscribed by President Cai Yuanpei. Prof. Jing Libin became the editor-in-chief. The journal was published by the National Peking University Press.

The emergence of the journal in natural sciences depends on the establishment of the universities and their progressing research in science and engineering. After the May 4th New Culture Movement, people's thoughts were greatly liberated. *The Science Quarterly of National University of Peking* spread and promote modern science and technology in China.

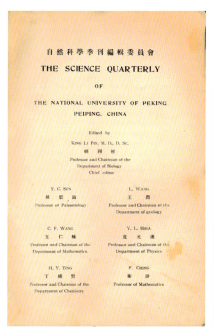

自然科学季刊编委会
Editorial Board of *The Science Quarterly*

自然科学季刊目录
Contents of *The Science Quarterly*

2.2.2《学海》杂志

数学是人类社会最古老的科学，在中国源远流长。到了近代，中国数学却与世界渐行渐远。1904 年，京师大学堂选派首批四十七人赴海外留学，冯祖荀被送往日本京都大学，成为中国留学专攻现代数学第一人。他与同学一起创办了"北京大学留日学生编译社"，并于 1908 年首发《学海》杂志，首篇即是冯祖荀翻译的"物质及以脱论"，其中采用了阿拉伯数字、现代数学符号和算式。作为中国最早的科技译刊之一，《学海》推动了现代科学在中国的传播。

1913 年秋，北大数学门首招两名新生，标志着中国现代第一个大学数学系（门）正式开始教学。继数学门后，现代科学的多个门类陆续在北大建立。中国社会数千年来经史子集独占学坛的局面被打破了，中国现代科学体制由此发端。

《学海》
Oceanus Scientiae

2.2.2 The Journal *Oceanus Scientiae*

The pursuit of mathematical truth has a long history in China. Pitifully, in pre-modern time, China lagged behind western countries in mathematics. However, in 1904, Imperial University of Peking sent 47 carefully-selected students and young scholars to study overseas. Among them, Feng Zuxun was sent to Kyoto University, and became one of the pioneers specializing in modern mathematics for China. Feng and his students founded the Compilation & Translation Society of Students from Imperial University of Peking in Japan, and in 1908 the Society published the inaugural issue of *Oceanus Scientiae* with its very first article "Matter and Ether" translated by Feng Zuxun where modern notation was adopted. As one of the earliest Chinese journals about translated works of science and technology, *Oceanus Scientiae* certainly contributed to the promotion of scientific propagation in China.

In fall 1913, Department of Mathematics at Peking University recruited 2 students. This marked the establishment of the very first mathematics department of Chinese higher education. Since then, other modern disciplines were founded at Peking University as well. Modern sciences began to develop in China.

《学海》
Oceanus Scientiae

2.2.3 "北京一号"和"红旗"计算机

计算机是20世纪最重要的科技发明之一。从最初的军用领域逐步扩展到社会的各个角落,计算机推动了世界范围的技术进步,引发了深刻的社会变革。

20世纪40年代,世界第一台计算机在美国问世,引起了中国的高度重视。50年代,学成归国的董铁宝是中国当时少有的亲自参与过相关研究的科学家,对中国计算机科学发展起到重要作用。1958年,北大计算数学教研室的张世龙带领王选等学生,与军方合作,自行设计研制了数字电子计算机"北京一号"并交付空军使用。之后,北大师生还参与了103计算机(中科院负责)和"红旗"计算机的研制工作,其中"红旗"计算机由北大自行设计,当时设定目标比苏联专家帮助研制的还高,最终于1962年试算成功。

1973年8月,北京大学电子仪器厂与北京有线电厂等单位合作在北大研制成功我国第一台每秒运算一百万次的集成电路电子计算机(简称"150机")。

王选(右)和同学及协作单位的同事在"北京一号"机前
Wang Xuan (Right) with His Peers and Colleagues in front of Beijing I Computer

讨论北大"红旗"计算机研制方案
Working on "Red Flag" Computer

2.2.3 "Beijing I" and "Red Flag" Computers

Computer is one of the most important technological innovations in the 20th century. From military applications to various other aspects of social life, computer profoundly changed the human life.

In the 1940's, the first computer was born in the United States. Certainly, China was highly aware of it. Dong Tiebao, returning to China following completion of his studies overseas, was one of the few experts with relative research experiences. Dong made key contributions to the development of computer science in China. In 1958, Zhang Shilong, then student Wang Xuan, and others from Peking University's computational mathematics group of the Department of Mathematics, independently designed and manufactured the digital "Beijing I" computer and transferred it to the air force. After that, Peking University also involved in the invention of the 103 computer (project led by the Chinese Academy of Sciences) and the "Red Flag" computer. The "Red Flag" computer successfully completed in 1962 was another autonomous masterpiece devised by Peking University, with higher standard than the one set by Soviet Union advisors.

Peking University and her local partners developed China's first computer "Model 150", to run at a million times per second in August, 1973.

图为工作人员正在调试 150 机
Testing 150 Computer

2.2.4 层子模型

探索物质的基本结构是自然科学研究的一个重要命题。在这项对人类智力极限的挑战中，来自北大的物理学家做出了可贵的贡献。1965 年到 1966 年，包括北大理论物理研究室专家在内的北京基本粒子理论组 39 人在分析了当时粒子物理理论和实验的问题后，提出了强子结构的层子模型。这些成果发表在《北京大学学报（自然科学版）》和《原子能》杂志上，同时在 1966 年的北京国际科学研讨会上做了专题报告。

层子模型认为，物质结构有无限的层次，在强子层次上的构成组分是层子，但层子并不是物质最终的组成部分，还可能包含更深层次的结构。囿于当时诸多因素，层子模型并未在国际学界得到广泛传播，而由两位美国物理学家稍早在大洋彼岸提出的夸克模型逐渐被广为接受。层子模型留在了中国一代物理学人的记忆深处。

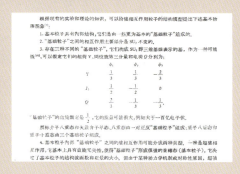

层子模型论文
Papers on the Straton Model

2.2.4 The Straton Model

To explore the fundamental structure of matter is one of the most critical problems in natural sciences, to which the scientists from Peking University made substantial contributions. From 1965 to 1966, the Beijing elementary particle theory group was established as a collaborative scheme of 39 Chinese physicists including the leading theorists from Peking University. Aiming to tackle the open questions in theories and experiments of particle physics, the group proposed a theoretical model, namely the straton model, to describe structure and property of hadrons. The research achievements led to a series of publications appeared in Chinese journals *Acta Scientiarum Naturalium Universitatis Pekinensis* and *Atomic Energy*, and were also presented in Beijing International Science Conference in 1966.

The straton model suggested that matter may be infinitely divisible, and stratons (also known as "quarks") could merely be the fundamental constituents at the level of hadrons. The research on the straton model was also one of the earliest attempts involving the quark dynamics, long before the commonly accepted model, quantum chromodynamics (QCD), showing that Chinese physicists were at the forefront of the particle physics research. Although the further development of the straton model was hindered by several reasons at the time, it remains a memorable landmark in the history of physics in China.

2.2.5 热力学与统计物理

热力学与统计物理在中国的建立和传播离不开北大物理系王竹溪。1938 年从剑桥大学博士毕业后，年仅 27 岁的王竹溪即被聘为西南联大物理系教授。他上课不带讲稿，却能将繁杂的公式和推演一字不差地写满黑板。杨振宁、李政道都是王竹溪的学生。他 1955 年编著的《热力学》是我国第一部热力学教材，他的《统计物理学导论》也是我国第一批理论物理教材之一。他与郭敦仁合著了《特殊函数概论》，其深厚的数学造诣令他得到国际数学界的敬重。

王竹溪不仅是科学大家，还有深厚的历史文化功底。他发明了汉字新部首检字法，花费了四十多年心血编纂出《新部首大字典》，收字超过 5.1 万字，篇幅达 250 万字之多。

王竹溪部分物理学著作
Some Physics Books Written by Wang Zhuxi

2.2.5 Thermodynamics and Statistical Physics

The advancement of research and education in thermodynamics and statistical physics in modern China cannot be fully portrayed without mentioning Professor Wang Zhuxi of Peking University. As a Ph.D. graduate from Cambridge University at 27 years old, Wang was appointed a professor of National Southwest Associated University in 1938. He became a professor of Peking University after the reorganization of the Chinese higher education system in 1952. Many students of Wang became world prominent physicists, such as C. N. Yang and T. D. Lee. Wang was known for giving rigorous derivations and thorough instructions in lectures without carrying any lecture notes. Wang authored several classical textbooks for physics education in China, such as *Thermodynamics* and *Introduction to Statistical Physics*. His work entitled *Special Functions* (co-authored with D. R. Guo) was further published in an English translation by World Scientific Publishing in 1989, and is highly valued as a systematic and instructive treatise for scientists in not only physics but also engineering and applied mathematics.

In the meantime, with a broad scholarly passion, Wang also remarkably made contributions to philology. Owing to his perseverance over more than 40 years, he succeeded in compiling one of the largest Chinese dictionaries featuring a unique radical indexing system of Chinese characters, which was published 5 years after his passing.

《新部首大字典》
New Radical Dictionary

2.2.6 微波辐射计

如何探测高空大气要素是一个极具挑战的科学难题。早在 20 世纪 50 年代，当时在苏联学习的赵柏林与领航员携带仪器乘气球飞至 1000—3500 米高空，进入云中测量电荷，开创了人类首次乘气球入云测量电荷的先例。然而，使用探空气球的弱点是无法得到时间上连续的气象要素资料，也无法测量云中的含水量。

1969—1978 年，在极其困难的条件下，北大物理系的赵柏林研制成功了多频微波辐射计系列（波长为 5 毫米—3 厘米，5 个波段），这一中国科学家的首创成果代表了当时世界的最高水平。1993—2003 年，以赵柏林为首席科学家的国际团队联合在淮河流域进行了能量与水分循环的观测研究，这是首次对梅雨期的淮河进行气象和水文联合观测研究，其间研制的微波辐射计在淮河流域洪水预报中发挥了良好作用。

微波辐射计
Microwave Radiometer

2.2.6 Microwave Radiometer

Monitoring weather, climate and environment is a scientific challenge. In 1950s, during his study in Russia, Professor Zhao Bolin of Peking University carried the equipment to a balloon up to the heights of 1000 – 3500 meters above ground, and accomplished mankind's first trial to measure charge in cloud by balloon. This approach, however, faced some limitations: in particular, it could neither provide the meteorological data with temporal continuity, nor allow the measurement of cloud water-content. Nevertheless, they became Zhao's motivation for further research in Peking University.

From 1969 to 1978, in spite of the particularly difficult conditions, Zhao successfully made outstanding breakthroughs by producing a series of multi-frequency microwave radiometers, with wavelengths from 5 mm to 3 cm and 5 wavebands, demonstrating one of the world's leading achievements in developing and utilizing atmospheric remote sensing instruments at the time. From 1993 to 2003, being the Chief Scientist, Zhao led an internationally collaborative program to conduct observations of energy and water cycle in the Huai River basin. This program was the first comprehensive meteorological and hydrological study of the Huai River basin during the rainy season, in which the self-developed microwave radiometers played a significant role in several aspects, such as the flood forecasting.

微波辐射计
Microwave Radiometer

2.2.7 稀土萃取分离

稀土有"工业维生素"之称，是 21 世纪最重要的战略资源之一。中国稀土储量占世界 70% 左右，然而一直没有突破生产技术这一难关。20 世纪 70 年代前，中国只能向国外廉价出口稀土原料，然后再高价进口深加工的稀土产品。"空有宝山，却受制于人"，这一令人扼腕叹息的局面被北大化学系徐光宪改变。

1972 年，徐光宪接受了研究生产稀土技术的紧急任务。他摒弃国际上通用的离子交换法，提出了萃取理论，并在此基础上设计出整套工艺流程。这一理论和方法大大提高了中国稀土工业的竞争力，使中国实现了从稀土"资源大国"到"生产大国"和"出口大国"的飞跃。2008 年，徐光宪荣获国家最高科学技术奖。

徐光宪与研究组同事
Xu Guangxian and His Colleagues

2.2.7 Rare Earth Extraction Separation

Regarded as "Industrial Vitamins", rare earth element is one of the most important strategic resources of the 21st century. China's rare earth reserves accounted for about 70% of the world's resources, however, there had been major limitations in the production technology. Before the 1970s, China could only export rare earth raw materials abroad, and then import high-grade rare earth products at high prices. This deplorable situation was changed by Xu Guangxian of the Department of Chemistry, Peking University.

In 1972, Xu Guangxian accepted the urgent research task of rare earth production technology. He abandoned the internationally common ion exchange method, put forward the extraction theory, and designed a complete set of process flow based on this theory. The extraction theory and method greatly improved the competitiveness of China's rare earth industry, and made China leap from the rare earth "resource power" to "production power" and "export power". In 2008, Xu Guangxian won the National Top Science and Technology Award.

国家最高科学技术奖证书
Certificate of National Top Science and Technology Award

2.2.8 人工合成结晶牛胰岛素

1965 年 9 月 17 日，中国科学家在世界上第一次用人工方法合成具有与天然分子相同化学结构和完整生物活性的蛋白质——结晶牛胰岛素，开辟了人工合成蛋白质的时代，在生命科学发展史上产生了重大意义与影响。在这一过程中，北大学者们留下了不可磨灭的印记。

这一研究始于 20 世纪 50 年代，北大先后有 300 余名师生参加了这项工作。1964 年至 1965 年，北大和中科院有机所、上海生化所在上海协同攻关。其中，北大团队在邢其毅等师生的努力下，与中科院有机所团队共同完成牛胰岛素 A 链的合成（上海生化所负责牛胰岛素 A、B 链拆合及 B 链的合成工作）。最终，A 链与 B 链相连成功，获得具有全部生物活性的牛胰岛素结晶。这一科学成果为中国赢得了世界的尊重，也标志着人类探索生命奥秘迈出了重要一步。

1982 年获国家自然科学一等奖后北大参与人员合影（前排居中者为邢其毅）
A Group Photo of National Science Award Team (Xing Qiyi in the Middle of the Front Row)

2.2.8 Synthetic Crystalline Bovine Insulin

On September 17, 1965, for the first time in the world, Chinese scientists completed total synthesis of crystalline bovine insulin, with the same chemical structure and complete biological activity of the natural protein. This work opened up the era of synthetic protein and made great significance and influence in the history of life sciences. Peking University scholars have left an indelible mark in this process.

This study began in 1950s, with the participation of over 300 professors and students from Peking University (PKU). During 1964 to 1965, scientists from Peking University, and the Institute of Organic Chemistry (IOC) and Shanghai Biochemical Institute (SBI) of Chinese Academy of Sciences carried out collaborative research in Shanghai. Under the efforts of Xing Qiyi and other professors and students, the PKU team and the IOS team together completed the synthesis of bovine insulin A chain (SBI team was responsible for the split of bovine insulin A, B chain and B chain synthesis). Eventually, the A chain was successfully linked to the B chain to obtain bovine insulin crystals with all biological activities. This scientific achievement brought China international respect, and also made an important step in the human exploration of the mystery of life.

北大化学系自 1958 年起开始人工合成牛胰岛素的研究。此为邢其毅（右一站立者）在指导人工合成牛胰岛素的研究
Xing Qiyi (right) and His Colleagues in the Experiment of Synthetic Crystalline Bovine Insulin

2.2.9 重水和稳定同位素

稳定同位素是自然科学研究的重要命题，在核工业等领域有重要应用。1991年，北大化学系的张青莲利用同位素质谱法测得铟元素的精确原子量（114.818±0.003），成为第一个被国际原子量表采用的由中国人测定的标准数据。

张青莲是中国稳定同位素学科的奠基人和开拓者。他1936年开始从事重水和稳定同位素研究，涉及氢、氧、碳、氮、锂、硼、硫、铟、锑、铕、铱等十几种元素的同位素。至2005年，他主持测定的铟、铱、锑、铕、铈、铒、锗、锌、镝等元素的相对原子质量新值，均被国际原子量委员会采用为国际新标准。

张青莲获奖证书
Award Certificate of Zhang Qinglian

2.2.9 Heavy Water and Stable Isotopes

Stable isotope is an important natural science research project, and has important applications in nuclear industry and other fields. In 1991, the exact atomic weight of indium (114.818 ± 0.003) was measured using isotope mass spectrometry by Zhang Qinglian, in Department of Chemistry, Peking University. It was the first standard data measured by a Chinese scientist that was adopted by the international atomic scale.

Zhang Qinglian is the founder and pioneer of China's stable isotope discipline. He began to work on heavy water and stable isotopes in 1936. His research involves isotopes of hydrogen, oxygen, carbon, nitrogen, lithium, boron, sulfur, indium, antimony, europium, iridium and other elements. In 2005, the new relative atomic mass values of indium, iridium, antimony, europium, cerium, erbium, germanium, zinc, dysprosium and other elements, which he led to determine, were all adopted as a new international standard by the International Atomic Quality Committee.

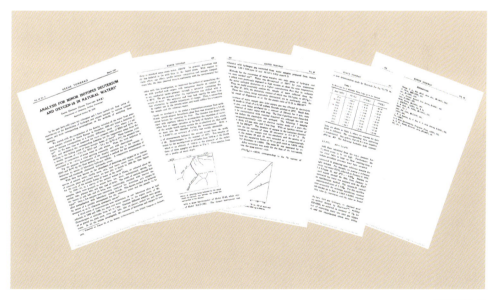

张青莲论文
Zhang Qinglian's Publications

2.2.10 北大地质博物馆

1931 至 1936 年，李四光出任北大地质学系主任。在任期间，他的一项重要举措是筹建北大地质馆。李四光利用自己的影响，联系社会各界募捐资金，并邀请著名建筑学家梁思成、林徽因进行地质馆的设计。地质馆 1934 年 5 月动工，1935 年 7 月竣工，落成在沙滩嵩公府夹道（现沙滩北街 15 号）。当时在地质馆第三层开辟了地质陈列室，是中国高校最早的地质博物馆。

1952 年院校调整期间，地质陈列室标本转移至新建的北京地质学院，1955 年在北大重建，1992 年迁入新地学楼（逸夫二楼）。目前的北大地质陈列馆，汇集了各类地质标本精华和世界各地典型地质标本 3000 余件。

建于 1935 年的北京大学地质博物馆
Geological Museum of Peking University, 1935

现在的北京大学地质博物馆
Current Geological Museum of Peking University

2.2.10 Geological Museum of Peking University

Li Siguang was dean of the Department of Geology, Peking University, from 1931 to 1936. In his term, the establishment of the geological museum was a priority on his agenda. He networked with famous architects Liang Sicheng and Lin Huiyin to design an uncompensated blueprint and other charitable individuals for endowments. Located at the Songgongfu street, Beach Avenue (present: 15 North street, Beach Avenue), the exhibition room was the earliest geological museum in Chinese universities. The construction work began in May,1934 and was completed in July,1935. The museum was relocated at the Department of Geology at the new campus in 1992 (No.2 Shao Yifu building). At present, the museum is home to a marvelous collection of more than 3000 pieces of geological specimens from around the world.

北京大学地质博物馆
Geological Museum of Peking University

2.2.11 莲花池与北京城河湖水系

北京城从何而来？

从西周初年的蓟城到金代的中都城，北京城址都位于今日北京城的西南、现莲花池以东的地区。虽然城市范围不断扩大，但原来的城址始终没有改变。这一城址的选择，与莲花池这个小湖泊以及由莲花池发源的一条小河（统称为莲花池水系）有密切关系。

元大都的兴建在北京城发展史上是一个重要转折点。它放弃了莲花池水系上历代相沿的旧址，而在它的东北郊外重建新城。新城城址以金代离宫——太宁宫附近的一区湖泊，即今日的中海和北海（当时南海尚不存在）为设计中心，而这片湖泊为高梁河水所灌注，属于高梁河水系。元代把北京城城址从莲花池转移到高梁河水系绝非偶然，而是出于城市建设的长远考虑。

把古代北京城市规划特点与地理环境分析结合起来，把古代城市规划思想放在地理环境的"地上"和河湖水系的"网上"来分析，并在此基础上揭示古代北京城"中轴线"所体现的"面南而王"思想的地理环境基础，这是侯仁之关于北京城市历史地理研究的重要贡献。

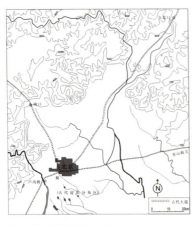

北京城起源的地理基础
The Geographical Basis of the Origin of Beijing City

北京周边原始水系分布图
The Distribution of Water System in the Surroundings of Beijing

2.2.11 Lotus Pond and Beijing River System

Where did the city of Beijing originate from?

Originated in the City of Ji in the early Western Zhou and the capital city in Jin Dynasty, the city of Beijing has been located in the southwest, an area to the east of Lotus Pond in modern times. Though under constant expansion, the old site of the city, built on a little stream originating in the Lotus Pond (the Lotus water system), has never changed.

The Dadu city in Yuan Dynasty, built anew at the northeast suburbs of the Lotus Pond, abandoned the old site dwelt by a succession of earlier dynasties to mark a turning point for the development of the city of Beijing. The new site is built along the new center — the Central Lake and the North Lake (the South Lake nonexistent) where lakes along Ligong and Tai Ninggong area were located in the Jin Dynasty. The lake poured by Sorghum River integrates into its water system. The relocation of Beijing city to the Sorghum River water system from the Lotus Pond is thus a long-term vision planned for the layout of the city rather than random.

Hou Renzhi has contributed significantly to the study of the historical urban geography of Beijing. His studies include: integration of the urban planning into geographical conditions, ancient urban planning ideology analysis by applying the ideology to the "ground" of the geographical environment and the "net" of river and lake system.

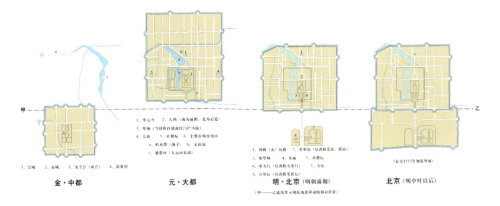

城址变迁——从莲花池水系到高梁河水系
Relocation of Beijing City: from Lotus Water System to Sorghum River Water System

2.2.12 地质素描图

王嘉荫，1935 年毕业于北大地质学系并留校任教，专长岩石学，是我国著名的岩石、矿物鉴定大师。

开卷必动笔是王嘉荫读书的习惯。不论读中文文献，还是英文、德文、俄文、日文等外文文献，他都习惯用英文记录下来。多年手记累积的厚度已超过 1 米，可惜在"文革"中全部遗失。在他生命的最后时期，王嘉荫已经重病缠身，但仍与病魔抢时间，不仅阅读了大量文献，而且观测了数百片岩石薄片。这些最后的手记成为他的珍贵遗物。图片所示是一部没有发表的地质学研究笔记，是王嘉荫一生从事地质教育科研工作的些许折射。

王嘉荫地质素描图
Geological Sketch by Wang Jiayin

2.2.12 Geological Sketch

A graduate of the Department of Geology, Peking University in 1935, Wang Jiayin stayed on to become a faculty member who had earned profound expertise in the field of rock and mineral identification.

It was Wang Jiayin's habit to note down what he read in English, whether the reading being in Chinese, English, German, Russian or Japanese. Over the years, his notes have accumulated a thickness of more than one meter, but unfortunately got lost during the "Cultural Revolution". Though seriously ill in the last years of his life, Wang Jiayin kept on reading and studied hundreds of pieces of rock. He left a precious relic of these notes to the world. The picture shows an unpublished geological study note — a reflection of Wang Jiayin's dedicated experience in geology education.

2.2.13 激光照排首张报纸样张

汉字是传承中华文明的重要载体。计算机发明后，如何处理汉字信息成为世界科技领域的一项重大挑战。20世纪80年代汉字激光照排系统的问世，带来了一场"告别铅与火、迎来电与光"的技术革命。该系统就源自于北大王选团队。

1975年，王选开始主持计算机汉字信息处理与激光照排系统的研究工作。1979年，在位于北大老图书馆（现档案馆）的机房里，王选用激光照排系统输出了第一张报纸样张——《汉字信息处理》。此后十余年，王选团队持续创新，使延续上百年的中国铅排印刷行业得到彻底改造，促成了电子出版这一新兴产业，占领了大陆99%的报业和80%的书刊（黑白）市场，以及海外80%的华文报业市场，被公认为"毕昇发明活字印刷术后中国印刷技术的第二次革命"。

今日，首张报纸样张依然保存在它诞生的地方——北大档案馆，静静地见证了这场伟大的革命。

汉字激光照排系统排印的首张报纸样张
The First Sample Newspaper Produced by the Chinese Character Laser Photo-typesetting System

王选在查看用激光照排输出的报纸胶片
Wang Xuan was Checking Newspaper Films Produced by Laser Photocopying

2.2.13 The First Sample Newspaper Produced by the Chinese Character Laser Photo-typesetting System

Chinese character is the indispensable vehicle that carries and inherits Chinese civilization. Ever since invention of the computer, the information processing of Chinese characters had been a gigantic challenge. In the 1980s, the Chinese character laser photo-typesetting system invented by Wang Xuan and his team from Peking University started a technological revolution which led China to bid farewell to the age of "Lead and Fire" and usher in the age of "Electronics and Light".

In 1975, Wang Xuan started to lead the research and development of Chinese character information processing and laser photo-typesetting system. In 1979, he succeeded in using the prototype to output the first sample newspaper, Chinese Character Information Processing, in the computer room of the former Peking University Library (currently the Archives of Peking University). During the following period of more than one decade, Wang Xuan and his team made innovations continuously, and completely revolutionized the industry of Chinese lead-type typography and printing which had lasted for hundreds of years. The new industry of electronic publishing took shape, and eventually occupied 99% of the market share of newspaper and 80% of that of books and magazines in mainland China, and 80% of that of oversea Chinese newspaper. It was universally recognized as "the second revolution of China's printing technology ever since Bi Sheng's invention of movable-type printing".

Today, the first sample newspaper is still preserved in the place where it was born—Archives of Peking University, which witnessed silently this great revolution.

2.2.14 战胜回归热

1935 年,北平(旧称,现北京)流行虱传播回归热,患者多为劳苦大众。北大医学院的钟惠澜为了研究这一问题,深入北平的贫民窟捕捉虱子进行调查。为了培养用于实验的活虱子,钟惠澜及助手以自己的身体作为试验品,供虱子叮咬吸血。钟惠澜对大量病虱进行剖验,在它们的唾液腺、卵巢、睾丸等器官内均未发现螺旋体。经过大量实验,他终于发现,人们是在挤碎虱子时被感染的——此时大量回归热螺旋体自虱体内逸出,经人们皮肤上的搔痕或叮咬伤口侵入而致病,从而推翻了教科书上"回归热是因感染性虱子吸人血而感染"的传统说法,对预防和治疗回归热做出了重要贡献。

钟惠澜在实验室
Zhong Huilan in Laboratory

2.2.14 Conquering Louse-borne Relapsing Fever

In 1935, louse-borne relapsing fever was prevalent in Peking (now known as Beijing), and the patients were mostly toiling people. In order to study the relapsing fever deeply, Zhong Huilan went into the slums to catch body lice and feed them on his own blood by letting the lice bite him. He examined large numbers of the infected lice and found no spiral in their salivary glands, ovaries, testes, and other organs. After numerous experiments, Zhong Huilan finally found relapsing fever was spread when the lice was crushed: During this process, *Borrelia recurrentis* was released from the lice, infected the person via mucous membranes in the scratched the area where the lice was feeding, and then invaded the bloodstream. This finding overthrew the theory from the traditional textbook "louse-borne relapsing fever is spread when the infected louse sucking blood". He made great contributions to the prevention and treatment of relapsing fever.

2.2.15 青蒿素的故事

2015年10月5日,历史翻开了新的一页。中国本土科学家全部在自己国家完成的工作第一次获得诺贝尔奖。她就是北大医学院1951级校友屠呦呦。

屠呦呦的研究领域是对疟疾寄生虫传染病的医治。疟疾是一种恶性度很高的传染病,在热带的亚洲、非洲、中南美洲广为流传。屠呦呦率领科研团队,通过数年的潜心研究,利用一种遍布于中国南北山野的植物青蒿,提取出具有强大的抑制疟原虫功能的青蒿素。此后,屠呦呦又合成出双氢青蒿素,其抗疟疗效为青蒿素的十倍。

青蒿素及其衍生物的发现与改进,挽救了中国与世界许多国家成千上万的生命。

屠呦呦在实验室
Tu Youyou in Laboratory

2.2.15 The Story of Artemisinin

History turned to a new chapter on Oct 15th, 2015. For the first time, Dr. Tu Youyou, educated at Peking University Medical College and employed in China, was awarded the Nobel Prize in Physiology or Medicine for her contribution in discovering therapeutic treatment of malaria, a malignant parasitic disease. Her team developed Artemisinin as an effective anti-malaria drug that saved millions of lives all over the world.

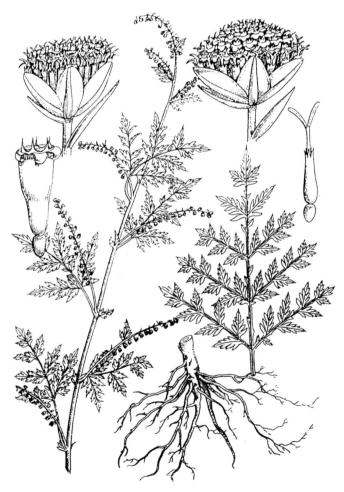

青蒿
Artemisia annua

2.2.16 中国第一例试管婴儿

1978年7月25日,世界第一例试管婴儿在英国诞生。这是人类生殖技术发展中的重要里程碑,给数百万不孕不育的夫妇带来了希望。

20世纪80年代,北京大学第三医院妇产科医生张丽珠研究了国外进展并结合中国国情,决定开展试管婴儿技术攻关。她带领的工作小组依靠了解的一些国外资料从零开始,经过13次试验,最终获得了妊娠成功。1986年3月10日,中国大陆第一例试管婴儿在北京大学第三医院诞生,标志着中国生殖技术短时间内追赶至世界先进水平。

此后,首例配子输卵管内移植婴儿、首例赠卵试管婴儿、首例冻融胚胎试管婴儿和首例代孕试管婴儿相继在北京大学第三医院诞生,为千家万户带来了福音。

张丽珠与首例试管婴儿(1988年)
Zhang Lizhu with the First IVF Baby in China (1988)

2.2.16 First IVF Baby in China

In 1986 when Chinese medical field was isolated from the world, Dr. Zhang Lizhu's team at Peking University Third Hospital successfully delivered the first healthy baby using in vitro fertilization technology. Since then, she and her successors have been leading the field of obstetrics and gynecology in China, benefiting millions of patients through innovative technology and outstanding medical services.

2.2.17 诺贝尔奖物理学奖得主崔琦与北大

2012年5月29日，1998年诺贝尔物理学奖得主、普林斯顿大学教授崔琦在北大接受名誉博士学位。在接受学位的讲话中，崔琦拿着一笔一画写下的讲稿，动情地回忆他与北大的缘分。

"我是在一个旧历年的时候，和父母亲告别，跟着一位在河南郑州纱布厂工作的表哥去郑州，经郑州来北京。记得我们年初六启程。步行三天，马车一天，第四天半夜到了京汉铁路的许昌站。因为是第一次离开农村，火车站在三更半夜叫我特别感到害怕、恐慌。幸亏，一上车就不同了，车里边样样都干净好看，我遇见了几位对我们很和睦的小伙子，他们都穿着整整齐齐的蓝色制服，很斯文、得意的样子。我和表哥一坐下来，表哥就给我细心地解释说他们不是当兵的，他们都是北大学生，过年后回北京念书的。他很郑重地对我说，我去到北京以后要好好努力读书，有一天幸运的话，可能也会像他们一样换上一套好看的中山装，做个北京大学的学生。我那时候听不懂他讲的内容，但是可感觉到他的好心话意。可能就是因为这几十年前在火车上的机遇，我后来总觉得和北大有缘分。"

2013年，崔琦与北大签订聘用协议，正式成为北大教授。他也成为北大全职聘用的第一位诺贝尔奖获得者。

崔琦在接受北大名誉博士授予仪式上的致辞（手稿）
Manuscripts of Daniel Tsui's Speech for Honorary Doctorate Ceremony of Peking University

2.2.17 Nobel Prize Laureate Daniel Chee Tsui's Story with Peking University

On May 29, 2012, 1998 Nobel laureate in physics, Princeton University professor Daniel Tsui received an honorary doctorate from Peking University. At the honorary ceremony, Daniel Tsui cordially shared his memories about Peking University.

I left home and followed my cousin towards Beijing. It was a very tough journey and my first time leaving home. In the middle of the night, the train station looked horrible. After we got on the carriage, everything became different, clean and nice. I met a few young people who were very kind, wearing neat blue uniform, gentle with proud looks. My cousin told me that they were not soldiers but students from Peking University. They went back home to spend the Chinese New Year with family and now on their way back to school. My cousin encouraged me to study hard and possibly become a Peking University student with nice uniform one day in the future. I could not understand what he was saying at that time, but could feel his kindness. Since then, I always feel there is a strong connection between Peking University and myself.

In 2013, Daniel Tsui signed an employment agreement with Peking University, and officially became a full professor at Peking University. He is also the first Nobel Prize winner to work full-time at Peking University.

崔琦与学生交流
Daniel Tsui in Classroom

Chapter Three
Gifts from Nature

第三章
自然的馈赠

燕园是有灵气的，这里不仅汇聚了中国建筑园林的巧思与精妙，近代中国最杰出学者的思想与创新，而且受到了大自然的格外关照与恩赐。当然，这依然是生活工作在这片独特土壤之上的人们用智慧与努力所带来的。第三章名为"自然的馈赠"，主要遴选了地质标本和植物样本两个部分。书中收录的地质标本是燕园学者在广袤的中国大地上寻觅探求的部分杰作，代表了北大在中国地质研究领域的成就与贡献，其中的大部分标本现藏于北京大学地质博物馆。植物标本也极具代表性，现藏于北京大学生命科学学院。风物、知识与馈赠，因为人的生生不息而使燕园的天地与历史、社会、自然产生了紧密和谐的关联。

Chapter Three: Gifts from Nature
第三章 自然的馈赠

Peking University campus has its soul. It not only brings together the ingenuity and exquisiteness of China's traditional architectures and gardens, the thoughts and innovations of the best scholars in modern China, but also received special care and gifts from the nature. Of course, all of these are the result of the wisdom and efforts of the people living and working here. The third chapter, entitled "Gifts from Nature", focuses on the selection of geological specimens and plant samples. The geological specimens are some representative masterpieces that Peking University scholars have discovered in the vast land of China, most of which are kept and exhibited in the Geological Museum of Peking University. Plant specimens are now stored in the School of Life Sciences. Because of people's efforts, the historical scenery, knowledge and natural gifts etc., have formed a close and harmonious relationship.

3.1 地质标本
3.1 Geological Specimens

3.1.1 世界上最早的蝾螈类化石

两栖动物是包括人类自身在内的脊椎动物家族中一个重要类群。两栖动物在地球生物演化系列中属于原始的四足动物，代表脊椎动物从水生到陆生重大历史演变过程中的一个关键环节。现生两栖动物包括有尾巴的蝾螈类、无尾巴的蛙类以及尾巴和四肢尽失的蚓螈类三个类群。

两栖类经历了漫长的演化历程，在身体结构上发生了极大分异：蛙类躯干极度缩短、后肢显著伸长，善于跳跃；蚓螈类身体拉长，彻底丢失了四肢。相比之下，蝾螈类则颇为保守地保持了原始四足动物的基本构造特征，成为研究两栖类乃至包括人类在内的四足动物起源的模式类群。

生物分类学上，以大鲵为代表的大约10%的蝾螈类属种被归入隐鳃鲵亚目（Cryptobranchoidea），而大约90%的现生蝾螈类则被归入蝾螈亚目（Salamandroidea）。蝾螈类这两个主要支系的分支分化是现代两栖类演化历史中意义非凡的事件，影响着其后一亿多年蝾螈类分类多样性的历史进程。

2012年中国辽西建平发现的侏罗纪北燕螈（*Beiyanerpeton*）化石代表迄今世界上发现的蝾螈亚目最早的化石记录。这一重要化石记录发现于建平的晚侏罗世髫髻山组（~ 157 Ma）地层中。此前欧洲早白垩世地层产出的最早记录为 ~ 114 Ma，而中国辽西的这一发现将蝾螈亚目的历史又推前了四千多万年。

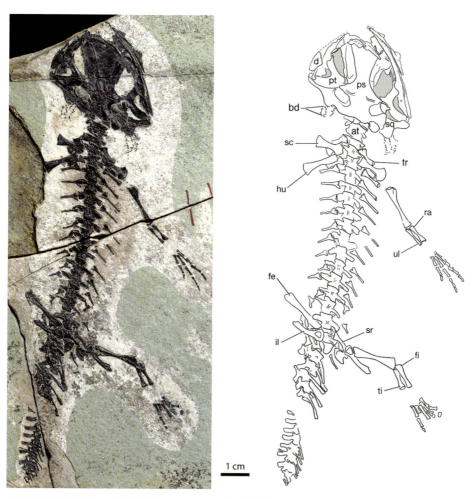

世界上蝾螈亚目最早的化石记录（157 Ma）——建平北燕螈（*Beiyanerpeton jianpingensis*）正型标本（PKUP V0601）腹面观（图件源于 Gao and Shubin，PNAS，2012）
Holotype (PKUP V0601) of *Beiyanerpeton jianpingensis*—the World's Oldest Fossil Record of Salamandroidea; Nearly Complete Skull and Postcranium in Ventral View (from Gao and Shubin, PNAS, 2012)

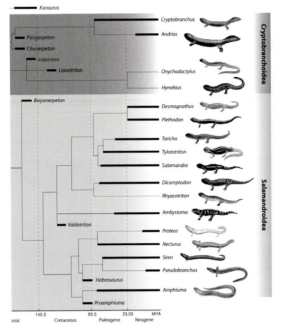

蝾螈类主要支系隐鳃鲵亚目与蝾螈亚目的分支演化关系图示。北燕螈位于蝾螈亚目最基部位置（图件源于 Gao and Shubin，PNAS，2012）
Evolution of Salamanders (From Gao and Shubin, PNAS, 2012)

辽西建平-北燕螈化石产地远景（图片中心平台为化石产出地点，建筑物为化石点保护工作站）
Beiyanerpeton Fossils from the Jurassic Beds in Jianping, Western Liaoning Province, China

3.1.1 Oldest Salamander in Earth History

Amphibians are an important taxonomic group among the vertebrates including humans ourselves. In the biological system on our Earth, amphibians are primitive tetrapods, representing a key link in the transition from water to land in the evolution of vertebrates. Living amphibians are known by three major subgroups: the tailed salamanders, the tailless frogs, and caecilians with no tail or limbs.

Undergone a long term evolution, the three subgroups of amphibians have evolved markedly different body plans: frogs display a greatly shortened trunk, but elongated hind limbs adapted for jumping; caecilians have an elongated body, and have the limbs entirely lost. In comparison, salamanders retained a body plan of primitive tetrapods, and thus are viewed as a model group for studying the origins of amphibians in particular, and the tetrapods in general.

In biological classification, approximately 10% of the salamander species including the giant salamanders are classified in the suborder Crytobranchoidea, with the remaining 90% being classified in the suborder Salamandroidea. The split of the two suborders is a major evolutionary event, as it had a pivotal impact on the evolution of salamanders for the over hundred million years thereafter.

In 2012, the discovery of *Beiyanerpeton* fossils from the Jurassic beds in Jianping, western Liaoning Province, documented so far the oldest fossil record of the Salamandroidea ever found. This key fossil discovery is made from the Late Jurassic Tiaojishan Formation, which has been dated at 157 million years. This fossil discovery predated the previously known record of 114 million years from the Upper Cretaceous of Europe by more than 40 million years.

3.1.2 世界上最早下海的鱼龙化石：2.48 亿年前三叠纪巢湖龙

巢湖龙（*Chaohusaurus*）是产于安徽巢湖地区早三叠世地层中的一种已绝灭的海生爬行动物，是目前世界上发现的最早的鱼龙。它体型较小、形态原始，成年个体身长 70—100 厘米，体形似鱼又似蜥蜴（龙），生活在距今约 2.48 亿年前（早三叠世）的温暖海洋中。

爬行动物是中生代（距今 2.52 亿年前至 6500 万年前）地球上的统治者。在 2.52 亿年前发生的二叠纪末期生物大绝灭事件导致古生代生态系统崩溃后，爬行动物迅速辐射演化，向入海、上天、占领整个陆地三大方向发展。进入海洋是爬行动物演化的重大事件，巢湖龙就是在这一重大生命演化事件产生的新的海洋生命的代表，填补了陆地祖先与完全适应海洋生活的鱼龙之间的演化环节。鱼龙由此出发，游向大洋，游向欧洲和北美，并最终称霸整个中生代的海洋。

作为最早从陆地进入海洋生活的爬行动物代表，巢湖龙曾被《科学》《自然》《美国国家地理》等报道和关注。图片展示的标本是北大地球与空间科学学院三叠纪海生脊椎动物研究团队于 2009 年 5 月在安徽巢湖马家山的发掘中获得。

巢湖龙 *Chaohusaurus* Young and Dong, 1972 化石标本及其复原图（藏于北大地质博物馆, 馆藏号：GMPKU-P-3086）
The Specimen and Reconstruction of *Chaohusaurus* Young and Dong, 1972 (GMPKU-P-3086, Geological Museum of Peking University)

3.1.2 The Earliest Ichthyosaur *Chaohusaurus* (Triassic, 248 Million Years Ago): First Marine Reptile Invasion into the Mesozoic Ocean

Chaohusaurus is an extinct Mesozoic marine reptile, found from the Lower Triassic at Chaohu of Anhui Province. It is known as the earliest ichthyosaur in the world, lived in the warm ocean in the Early Triassic, about 248 million years ago. The body shape of *Chaohusaurus* looks like fish somehow but still maintain some lizard features, and the body length of the adult is about 70 – 100 cm, which is quite small and primitive among ichthyosaurs.

The reptiles were the top predators in the Mesozoic (from 252 million years ago to 65 million years ago). They radiated rapidly after the collapse of the Paleozoic ecosystem resulted from the end-Permian mass extinction, diversifying into the ocean, the sky and the whole continent. It was a major bioevent in the evolutionary history of reptiles that they invaded into the Mesozoic ocean. *Chaohusaurus* was a representative species evolved in this event, which linked the evolutionary stage between its terrestrial ancestors and the typical cruise ichthyosaurs. From here, the ichthyosaurs swam to the open ocean, to Europe and North American, and dominated the Mesozoic ocean eventually.

As the earliest representative of the Mesozoic marine reptiles, *Chaohusaurus* were reported by *Science*, *Nature* and *National Geographic*. This specimen was excavated from Majiashan Quarry, Chaohu by the Triassic Marine vertebrate research team of School of Earth and Space Sciences, Peking University in May, 2009.

3.1.3 最早的植物根茎化石

根系是植物与外部环境相互作用的直接媒介。然而，早期植物的根系化石非常少见，这制约着人们对早期陆地生态系统中植物与土壤相互作用的认识。北大地质系古植物学课题组经过多年的野外调查，于 2010 年在云南曲靖地区发现已知最早的植物根系化石（距今 4.1 亿年）——胜峰工蕨（*Zosterophyllum shengfengense*）的簇生根。这种古老的根仅占整体植物生物量不到 3%，如此小的根系能够为相对较大的茎轴系统有效提供养分，表明早期植物具有较强的根系吸收能力和水分利用效率。2016 年，该团队在同一地区的稍晚地层中发现最早的具根系古土壤。一类原始的维管植物——曲靖镰蕨（*Drepanophycus qujingensis*）——在土壤形成和地貌稳定过程中起到关键作用。镰蕨可通过地下的根状茎克隆生长，形成长寿克隆体。庞大的根状茎系统可增进河流沉积物的抗侵蚀能力、促进成土作用，从而增强河流地貌的稳定性，提高早期土壤的固碳能力。这些化石发现对研究早期植物对地球系统演化的影响提供了非常有价值的参考。

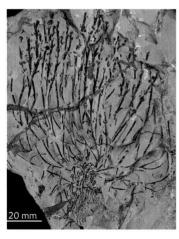

最早的具根系植物——胜峰工蕨（*Zosterophyllum shengfengense*）（藏于北大地质博物馆）
The Earliest Known Plant with a Rooting System (Geological Museum of Peking University)

距今 4.1 亿年的原始土壤与植物根状茎化石（单个根状茎宽度约 10 mm）（藏于北大地质博物馆）
The Primary Soil and Root Fossil (>410 Ma)(the Width of Roots are about 10 mm) (Geological Museum of Peking University)

3.1.3 Fossils of the Earliest Known Rooting Systems

Plants interact directly with the outside environments by their rooting systems. However, root fossils of the early plants are rarely documented, hindering a better understanding of the plant-soil interactions in early terrestrial ecosystems. Through careful fieldwork during the past years, the paleobotanic research team of the Department of Geology, Peking University, has discovered the earliest known rooting system from 410-million-year-old deposits of Qujing, Yunnan Province, China. This rooting system represents the fibrous roots of an early vascular plant, *Zosterophyllum shengfengense*. Such roots constitute only ca. 3% of the total biomass of the plant. The small rooting system was able to supple sufficient nutrients to the relatively large shoot system, suggesting a strong uptake capacity and high water use efficiency. In 2016, this team documented the earliest rooted paleosols (fossil soils) from the deposits of a slightly younger age in the same area. A primitive vascular plant, *Drepanophycus qujingensis*, has been demonstrated to play essential roles in the soil formation and landscape stabilization. This plant can produce large long-lived clones via the clonal growth of belowground rhizomes. Rhizome networks contributed to the accumulation and pedogenesis of fluvial sediments and furthermore, to the increasing stability of river banks and floodplains. The discovery of these fossils sheds lights on the studies of the impact of early plants on the evolution of the earth system.

3.1.4 神奇的拖鞋珊瑚化石

拖鞋珊瑚是非常独特的珊瑚化石：尖头微翘，形如拖鞋，半圆形萼盖沿直边开合，还可能随水流在海底旋转，近四亿年前在中泥盆世广见于亚欧、北美和大洋洲。乐森璕所著的《拖鞋珊瑚的新分类及其地质分布》（1978 年），为解决国际争论提出了重要见解。

乐森璕 1924 年毕业于北大地质学系，从事地质科学和地质教育六十余年，在四射珊瑚及泥盆系地层研究中颇有建树，如 1937 年刊于德国著名的《古生物学会志》的论文《广西中泥盆世珊瑚动物群》。他构建了中国泥盆系下、中统地层格架，创建了下二叠统茅口组及中泥盆统东岗岭组等著名地层单位。他与吴望始合著的《珊瑚化石（四射珊瑚）》（1964 年），全面总结并修订了国际分类。他关于西藏南部中生代六射珊瑚的研究，填补了学术空白并确定了地层时代。

拖鞋珊瑚化石（藏于北大地质博物馆）
Slipper Coral Fossils (Geological Museum of Peking University)

3.1.4 Magical Slipper Coral Fossils

Slipper coral is a very unique coral fossil: pointedly tilted, shaped like slippers, with the semicircle calyx lid opening and closing along the straight line. It also makes seabed rotation with sea wave. About 400 million years ago, the Middle Devonian, Asia, Europe, North America and Oceania were populated by slipper coral. Yue Senxun's *New Classification of Slipper Coral and its Geological Distribution* (1978) shed important insights into the related international dispute.

Yue Senxun, who graduated from the Department of Geology, Peking University in 1924, has been engaged in geology research and education for more than 60 years. In particular, he has contributed to the research of the strata of coral and Devonian, such as publishing *Guangxi Middle Devonian Coral Fauna*, in 1937 in Germany's famous periodical *Paleontology Society*. He constructed the formation of the lower and middle strata in China, and established the formation of the Permian Mao Kou Group and the Middle Devonian East Hillock Ridge Group. Yue Senxun and Wu Wangshi published *Coral Fossils (Tetracoral)* (1964) in which a comprehensive summary and revision of the international classification is provided. His study of the Mesozoic Hexacoral in southern Tibet filled the academic gap and determined the stratigraphic age.

3.1.5 中国蓝片岩

蓝片岩是板块俯冲过程中形成的低温高压变质岩，通常被认为是板块俯冲带的标志。中国发育着多条蓝片岩带，最年轻的是雅鲁藏布江蓝片岩带，最古老的是阿克苏前寒武纪蓝片岩带。在这一研究过程中，北大的董申保最早开展中国蓝片岩系统研究工作并提出：蓝闪石片岩不仅限于是洋壳俯冲的产物，它也可能出现在陆壳环境中，并以形成蓝闪绿片岩相为特征。他通过对扬子克拉通北缘蓝片岩和榴辉岩的研究，建立了陆壳俯冲型高压变质作用成因模型，得到国际地质学界的广泛关注和引用。

中国北祁连山蓝片岩（a）和新疆阿克苏蓝片岩（b）（藏于北大地质博物馆）
Blueschist from North Qilian Mountains (a) and from Aksu in Xinjiang (b) (Geological Museum of Peking University)

3.1.5 Chinese Blueschist

Blueschist, viewed in general as an indicator of plate subduction zone, is a low temperature and high pressure metamorphic rock formed by plate subduction. China has developed many blueschist belts, the youngest of which is the Yarluzangbo River blueschist belt, and the oldest of which is the Aksu Precambrian blueschist belt. Dong Shenbao of the Peking University started the research work of the Chinese blueschist and proposed that the genesis of the Blueschist does not arise in the oceanic crust subduction alone. It may also appear in the continental crust setting, and it is characterized by the greenschist-facies retrograde overprint. Based on the study of the blueschist and eclogite in the northern margin of the Yangtze craton, a continental subduction model for blueschists formation during high pressure metamorphism is proposed, which arouses the attention and references of the international geologists.

3.1.6 白云鄂博的稀土矿标本：世界最大稀土矿的发现

1927 年，28 岁的丁道衡随中国西北科学考察团在绥远省达尔罕旗（今内蒙古包头市达尔罕茂明安联合旗）百灵庙以西 40 千米发现了白云鄂博铁矿并采集了十几箱矿石标本。1933 年结束考察后，返回北京的丁道衡委托何作霖对白云鄂博矿石进行研究。

何作霖把丁道衡采集的矿石标本制成薄片，在显微镜下发现铁矿石里的紫色萤石有一些褪色的小白点。他发现这些白点里有两种细小矿物，经中央研究院物理研究所光谱分析，证明是稀土矿物独居石和氟碳钙锦矿。1935 年,《中国地质学会会志》第 14 卷第 2 期刊登了何作霖编著的《绥远白云鄂博稀土类矿物的初步研究》（英文），第一次向世界宣告：白云鄂博矿物中存在稀土矿物。

1958 年，中国科学院与苏联科学院组成联合考察队，研究白云鄂博矿的物质组成。经过几年艰苦努力后终于查明，这一矿山是世界上最大的稀土矿。

白云鄂博的稀土矿床露天采场
Mining Field of Bayan Obo Rare Earth Ore Deposit

3.1.6 Rare Earth Mineral Specimen from Bayan Obo Ore Deposit: Discovery of the World's Largest Rare Earth Ore Deposit

In 1927, the 28-year-old Ding Daoheng, a team member of the Northwest China Scientific Expedition to Suiyuan Province (present: Darhan Muminggan Lianheqi, Baotou, Inner Mongolia) discovered the Bayan Obo ore deposit and collected more than 10 cases of ore mineral specimens, 40 kilometers to the west of the Lark Temple. When Ding Daoheng returned to Beijing after the investigation in 1933, the relevant research was handed over to He Zuolin.

With the ore mineral specimens collected by Ding Daoheng made into thin sections, He Zuolin found some faded small white spots in iron ore purple fluorite under the microscope. He found that there were two small minerals in those white spots, monazite and parasite which were proved by the spectrum analyses in National Research Institute of Physics, Academia Sinica. In 1935, the 2nd issue of the 14th volume of the Journal of *The Chinese Society of Geological Sciences* published "A Preliminary Study on the Rare Earth Minerals at Bayan Obo Ore Deposit" in English. In the paper, the author, He Zuolin, for the first time in the related field in the world, argued that there are rare earth minerals at Bayan Obo ore deposit.

In 1958, the Chinese Academy of Sciences and the Soviet Academy of Sciences formed a joint expedition to study the chemical composition of Bayan Obo ore deposit. After years of hard work, it was proven the largest rare earth mine of its nature in the world.

稀土矿物独居石
Rare Earth Material Monazite

3.1.7 北大的地热井

地热是可利用的清洁能源，也是重要的地球物理场之一，从一个侧面记录了地球形成和演化的历史。

20世纪60年代后期，李四光以远见卓识和对国家科技政策的影响力，倡导开展地热地质研究。北大地质地理系率先在国内开展此类工作。1970—1972年期间，北大与有关单位合作，对京津地区的地热资源进行调查，并在河北省怀来县后郝窑开展地热发电实验，成功利用86度的低温地热，建立了我国第一个地热实验电站（200千瓦）。1973—1974年间，北大地热组与有关单位对腾冲地区的火山活动与地热资源进行联合勘查，提出腾冲热海地热田是一个高温湿蒸汽田，发电能力可达10万千瓦。

在推动国家利用地热资源的同时，研究团队也造福了北大自身。2004年，北大在静园成功建设了第一口地热井，2006年又在中关新园建设了第二口地热井。

北大第一口地热井
The First Geothermal Well at Peking University

3.1.7 Geothermal Wells at Peking University

Geothermal resources is an available clean energy and one of the most important geophysical fields, which records the history of Earth's formation and evolution from one aspect.

In the late 1960s, Li Siguang advocated the study of geothermal geology with his foresight and influence on national science and technology policy. The Department of Geology and Geography, Peking University, took the lead in carrying out such work in this country. During 1970 – 1972, Peking University cooperated with other institutions to investigate the geothermal resources of Tianjin, and carried out geothermal power experiments in Huailai County, Hebei Province, and successfully used 86 degrees of low-temperature geothermal energy to establish the first geothermal experimental power station in China (200 kW). In 1973 – 1974, the geothermal group of Peking University and cooperative institutions conducted a joint exploration of volcanic activity and geothermal resources in Tengchong area, and proposed that Tengchong geothermal field was a high temperature and humidity steamed field with a generating capacity up to 100 000 kW.

While promoting the use of geothermal resources in the country, the research team also benefited the university itself. In 2004, Peking University successfully built the first geothermal well in Jingyuan, a garden on the campus of Peking University, and in 2006, the second geothermal well was built in the new Zhongguan park.

第二口地热井
The Second Geothermal Well at Peking University

3.1.8 岫岩玉：人类最早的玉石器件（8000年前）

河磨玉，俗称岫岩软玉，是由透闪石组成的玉石。虽然主要产自辽宁岫岩县，但与岫岩玉（蛇纹石玉）不同的是，河磨玉比重较大，硬度也较高，质地细腻，与著名的和田玉同质，属高档玉石，价值远高于岫玉。根据与出土文物对比和古文献记载，我国新石器时代（10 000—4000 年前）的几千年发展历史中，古玉用料主要来源于北方岫岩的河磨玉——从 8000 年前的兴隆洼文化到红山文化、后红山文化，山东的大汶口文化到龙山文化等均是如此。

河磨玉的发现是由北大地质系师生长期开展岫岩玉研究基础上完成的。在大量古文献和出土文物记载基础上，结合矿物学研究，北大师生确定河磨玉是人类使用最早的玉石，至今已有 8000 年历史。

河磨玉原料（藏于北大地质博物馆）
Primary Hemo Jade (Geological Museum of Peking University)

3.1.8 Xiuyan Jade: the Earliest Article of Jade Made by Human Beings (8000 Years Ago)

Hemo Jade, commonly known as Xiuyan nephrite, is jade composed of tremolite.

Though the Hemo Jade is mainly found in Xiuyan, Liaoning Province, it is different from Xiuyan Jade (serpentine jade) in that the Hemo Jade has a higher density, solid hardness and a delicate texture which is of the same nature with Hetian Jade. It is high-graded with a value far outweighing Xiuyan Jade.

The discovery of the Hemo Jade, was made after many years' research on Xiuyan Jade by the Department of Geology, Peking University. Hemo Jade is the earliest Jade (>8000 years) used by human beings 8000 years ago. This conclusion was made by the professors in Department of Geology, Peking University, based on both mineral analyses and archaeological literatures.

雕饰品
Art Jade

3.1.9 野外笔记

谢家荣（1898—1966），地质学家、矿床学家、地质教育家，1955 年首批中国科学院地学部委员（院士）。他曾几度在北大任教，1936—1937 年任北大地质学系主任，对北大地质学系的建设和地质人才的培养做出了重要贡献。

早在 20 世纪 20 年代，谢家荣就在北大地质学系担任教职。1925—1927 年，他为地质学系的学生讲授"经济地质学"和"中国矿产专论"，并于 1936—1937 学年任地质学系主任。这期间谢家荣对地质学系的课程进行了调整，确定了全系的必修课和选修课，三、四年级不再分设古生物学、矿物岩石学、经济地质学三个学门。此外，还规定学生须修习第一外国文（英文）一年，第二外国文（德文或法文）两年，但此项课程本系不计学分。四年级学生需做毕业论文。这些改革为后来地质学系的发展奠定了基础。

新中国建立后，谢家荣在地质部工作。协助李四光和黄汲清一道组织开展我国的石油普查勘探工作，为新中国发现大庆油田做出了杰出贡献。

谢家荣对北大深有感情，他的工作记录等文件存放在北大档案馆。2002 年编的"谢家荣教授人物档案目录"里收录了 1187 件，包括谢家荣的野外笔记本、野外记录册、书信、外文笔记本、科学论文的手稿等等。

谢家荣手稿
The Manuscript of Shei Jiarong

3.1.9 Shei Jiarong's Field Work Notes

Shei Jiarong (1898 – 1966), geologist, mineral deposit scientist, geology educator, and academician (1955) of the Chinese Academy of Sciences. Once taught at Peking University, he was the Director of the Department of Geology of Peking University in 1936 – 1937 and was dedicated to the development of the Department of Geology and the cultivation of the geological talents.

As early as in the 1920s, Shei Jiarong was in the Faculty of Geology at PKU. He lectured "Economic Geology" and the "China Mineral Monograph" for students of the Department of Geology from 1925 to 1927. During the time when he was dean of the department in the 1936 – 1937 school year, the curriculum of the Department of Geology was adjusted; the compulsory courses and elective courses were determined, and the three or four grade is no longer divided into three studies of paleontology, mineralogy, and economic geology. In addition, students were required to practise the first foreign language (English) for one year, and the second foreign language (German or French) for two years. However, this course did not count credits. Senior students were required to do academic theses for graduation. These reforms laid the foundation for the later development of the Department of Geology.

After the founding of New China, Shei Jiarong worked in the Ministry of Geology. He assisted Li Siguang and K.T. Huang to carry out the oil survey and exploration work in China, and contributed significantly in the discovery of Daqing oilfield.

Shei Jiarong has strong emotional bond with Peking University. His work records, including "Professor Shei Jiarong's Profile Directory" 2002, totaling 1187 documents, are stored in the Archives of Peking University. His field notebooks, field records, letters, notebooks in foreign languages and his manuscripts of scientific papers are among the collections.

3.2 植物样本
3.2 Plant Samples

3.2.1 中国遗传学的第一个教学工具

遗传学是生命科学最主要的支柱学科。在西方以孟德尔、摩尔根为杰出的先行者代表。中国的遗传学研究则是由李汝祺开创并建立的。

李汝祺在美国普渡大学获得博士学位后进入哥伦比亚大学，在当时动物系主任、细胞学家 E.B. 威尔逊和实验胚胎学家 T.H. 摩尔根的指导下从事遗传学方面的研究。1927 年，李汝祺回国担任燕京大学生物系教授，后来在北京大学生物系任教。他把经典遗传学引入了中国，并培养了刘承钊、谈家桢、张作干、金荫昌、李肇特等一批一流学者，使遗传学在中国传播、开花和结果。

图片所示为李汝祺从美国带回国用于遗传学教学的玉米。

3.2.1 The First Genetics Teaching Demonstration in China

Genetics is one of the most important branches of biological sciences, established by pioneers such as Gregor Mendel and T.H. Morgan. Genetics was established in China by Li Ruqi who obtained his Ph.D. training with T.H. Morgan. Li Ruqi trained the first group of students in genetics who later all became outstanding scientists. The photo shows the corn that Li Ruqi brought back to China as a teaching demonstration.

李汝祺从美国带回用于遗传学教学的玉米
The Corn that Li Ruqi Brought Back to China as a Teaching Demonstration

3.2.2《中国模式标本照片集》

生物多样性研究很重要的一个方面是志书的编撰，如植物志、动物志及菌物志等。中国的生物多样性研究最早始于欧洲和美国科学家所做的工作，他们从17世纪中期就开始进行非法标本采集，一直延续到1949年中华人民共和国成立。很多在华的外交官、传教士和一些专门的植物猎人在中国山区采集了大量的生物标本，也使大量的标本保存在欧美的各大自然历史博物馆里，欧美植物学家研究了其中的很多标本，并以之为凭证标本发表了很多有关新种的论文。

20世纪初，当中国植物学者开始研究中国生物多样性并着手编写中国植物志的时候，这些凭证标本是需要参考的重要材料，但囿于经费和语言等原因，许多中国植物学家不能直接到国外查看这些标本，给我国的研究造成了非常大的困难。中国植物分类学先辈秦仁昌在胡先骕（中国植物分类学奠基人、静生生物调查所所长、北京大学兼职教授）和中华教育文化基金董事会的资助下，于1931—1932年到欧洲各大标本馆进行拍摄收集。这些照片在当年冲洗出来几套，北大收存了一套。因此，这套《中国模式标本照片集》也已经有85年的历史了，它在中国植物志的编写和中国的植物多样性研究中起到了不可估量的重要作用。

作为中国著名植物学家、中国蕨类植物学的奠基人，秦仁昌于1940年发表的《水龙骨科的自然分类系统》解决了当时世界蕨类植物系统分类中最大的难题。这个分类系统是世界蕨类植物系统分类发展史上的一个重大突破，后来被国际上称为"秦仁昌系统"。

1993年，秦仁昌获得国家自然科学一等奖。

3.2.2 The First Botanical Encyclopedia in China—*Flora of China*

The classification of plants is a crucial issue in the history of life sciences. *Flora of China* (*Flora Reipublicae Popularis Sinicae*), the first botanical encyclopedia in China, has played a significant role in promoting botanic studies in China and the world.

Ching Renchang, the editor-in-chief of this book, is a famous Chinese botanist and the founder of ferns studies in China. He published *On Natural Classification of the Family "Polypodiaceae"*, solved the most challenging problem in ferns taxonomy at that time, which was known as the "Ching System".

In 1993, Ching Renchang was awarded the first-class honor of National Natural Science Awards in China.

中国模式标本照片
Album of Chinese Plants Type Specimens (Ching Renchang)

3.2.3 百年标本

这是 1905 年京师大学堂时期的标本，也是中国学者最早采集的植物标本。它是京师大学堂时期的博物实习科在日本教员指导下于北京百花山采集的。

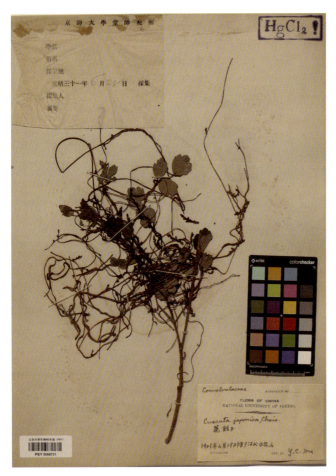

在百花山采集的植物标本
Plant Sample Collected on the Baihua Mountain

3.2.3 The Earliest Plant Specimens Collection Study in China

This is a plant specimen collected in 1905, the earliest one for scientific study in China. It was collected on the Baihua Mountain under the guidance of a Japanese instructor by students during the period of the Imperial University of Peking, the former name of Peking University.

石竹
Dianthus Chinensis L.

3.2.4 钟观光植物标本

钟观光，中国近代植物分类学的开拓者和奠基人。他是中国用近代植物分类学方法研究和进行大规模系统化植物采集的第一人。在北大任教期间，钟观光进行了系统的植物标本采集研究工作，曾立下"欲行万里路，欲登千重山。采集有志，尽善完成"的誓言。在4年时间里，他的足迹遍布11个省区，北尽幽燕，南至滇黔，行程万里，采集植物标本15 000余号。他领导创建了中国最早的植物标本室——北大植物标本室和中国第一个近代植物园——杭州笕桥植物园。

在现在植物分类体系中，以纪念钟观光命名的植物有19种，目前北大生物标本馆保存了4500多份钟观光采集的植物标本。

钟观光采集的标本：钟君木（假紫珠）
Tsoongia axillariflora Merr. A Specimens Collected by Tsoong Kuan-Kuang

3.2.4 Plant Specimens Collected by Tsoong Kuan-Kuang

Tsoong Kuan-Kuang, pioneer and founding person of plant classification in China, was the first Chinese scientist who systematically collected more than 15 000 plant specimens from more than 11 provinces in China.

In the current plant classification system, 19 plants were named in honor of Tsoong Kuan-Kuang. In the PKU Biological Specimen Depository, over 4000 plant samples were collected by him.

钟观光（1869—1940，钟任建提供）
Tsoong Kuan-Kuang (1869 – 1940, Provided by Zhong Renjian)

3.2.5 吴韫珍手绘《中国植物图谱》

形态学和分类学是历史上生物学研究的重要内容，细致的绘画描述是主要的展现手段。中国第一本综合现代植物分类图谱——长达 10 卷的《中国植物图谱》包括了近 2000 种华北和云南高原植物的精细解剖图和植物冬芽形态图，此套图谱不仅收录植物种类全面，而且观察细致、画图精美、注解详细，具有极高的科研和历史价值。它的作者叫吴韫珍（1899—1941），是中国植物分类学的奠基人之一。

吴韫珍 1927 年在美国康乃尔大学获得博士学位后回国，主要从事华北植物的调查和分类。他从事科研、教学工作，培养出包括吴征镒在内的一批著名植物学学者。1938 年，吴韫珍在滇西大理和鸡足山采集时由于过于辛劳，胃病复发转为腹膜炎而于 1941 年英年早逝。

1946 年，北京大学与清华大学的植物标本室合并成为北大生物系植物标本室。之后，吴韫珍手绘的《中国植物图谱》一直保存于其中。

《中国植物图谱》吴韫珍绘
Atlas of Plants in China by Wu Wenchen

3.2.5 The Illustration of Chinese Plants

Morphology and taxonomy were essential approaches in the history of biological sciences. Drawings and paintings were common methods of study. Wu Wenchen (1899 – 1941) was the pioneer in establishing these modern scientific methods in China, after receiving a Ph.D. from Cornell University. His fieldwork covered a wide area of China, collected and classified more than 2000 plant species. This line of research resulted in a ten volume of Atlas of Plants in China. Extremely harsh fieldwork condition in war-ridden China and meager medical treatment brought this brilliant scientist's life to a tragic end in 1941.

吴韫珍（1899 – 1941）（植物分类学家匡可任绘于 1941 年）
Wu Wenchen (1899 – 1941)(Painted by Plant Taxonomist Kuang Keren, 1941)

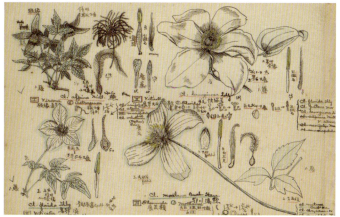 

植物手绘
Drawings of Plants

Chapter Four
Safeguard of Civilization

第四章
文明的守护

Treasures of Yan Yuan
燕园珍藏

坐落于北京大学西校门内清代鸣鹤园旧址中的北京大学赛克勒考古与艺术博物馆,由美国友人赛克勒夫妇捐资兴建,其中珍藏着原燕京大学、老北京大学,和1952年后北京大学考古专业的师生历年田野发掘、社会捐赠的珍贵文物近两万件,其中不乏精品。

北京大学图书馆源自于1898年的京师大学堂藏书楼,百余年来北京大学图书馆经过几代人的努力,形成了宏大丰富、学科齐全、珍品荟萃的馆藏体系,目前的文献资源累积已经达到1100余万册,其中包括150万册中文古籍。外文善本、金石拓片、1949年前出版物的收藏量均居全国图书馆前列。

这一部分选择的文物和文献资料,从来源上说,分别来自于原燕京大学、老北京大学、新中国成立后北京大学的收藏;从时间上来说,涵盖了不同历史阶段的代表性作品。

北大赛克勒考古与艺术博物馆
Arthur M. Sackler Museum of Art and Archaeology at Peking University

Chapter Four: Safeguard of Civilization
第四章 文明的守护

Arthur M. Sackler Museum of Art and Archaeology at Peking University sits at the old site of the Mingheyuan of the Qing Dynasty near the University's western gate on campus. Funded by the Sacklers from the U.S., the Museum houses approximately 20 000 pieces of cultural heritage from donation and field excavation by professors and students from Yenching University, old Peking University and the Department of Archaeology, Peking University, established in 1952. There are quite a number of precious collections.

Peking University Library grew out of the library of the old Imperial University of Peking established in 1898. With efforts of generations of librarians, the Library today boasts a variety of collections and resources, covering diverse subjects, distinguished especially with its rich collection of treasures and rare items. So far, the Library has collected over 11 million monographs, including 1.5 million ancient Chinese books. The Library ranks among the forefront in China, in terms of the collection of rare foreign-language books, rubbings of stele and bronze inscriptions, and publications before 1949.

The collections and documents presented in this chapter, come from former Yenching University, the old Peking University and Peking University, They are representative objects of different historical periods.

北京大学图书馆
Peking University Library

4.1 文物聚珍

4.1 Collections of Cultural Relics

4.1.1 "金牛山人"头骨

　　1984年9月27日至10月6日,在辽宁营口县金牛山的洞穴堆积中,发现了50余件人类化石。其中有较完整的头骨、脊椎骨、肋骨、尺骨、髋骨、髌骨、手骨和足骨等50余件,属于一个青年男性个体。同时出土了许多打制石器和部分骨器,以及用火的痕迹。

　　"金牛山人"生存的地质时代为中更新世晚期,距今28万年左右。"金牛山人"的头骨壁厚度小于北京猿人而大于现代人,代表了从直立人向早期智人过渡的中间类型。"金牛山人"化石的发现填补了这一时期人类发展的空白,为探讨人类起源和发展提供了重要材料。

4.1.1 Skull of Jinniushan Man

From September 27 to October 6, 1984, more than 50 human fossils were found in the Cave of Jinniu Mountain in Yingkou county, Liaoning Province. There are a complete skullcap, a backbone, ribs, an ulna, a hipbone, a patella, and bones from hands and feet. All of the remains belong to a young adult male. At the same time archaeologists unearthed a number of chipped stone tools and some bone tools, and also some traces of fire.

Jinniushan man lived in the geological age of the late Pleistocene that is about 280 000 years ago. His skull wall is thinner than that of the Beijing man, but thicker than the modern people. It represents a hominid type that falls between *Homo erectus* and early *Homo sapiens*. The discovery of Jinniushan fossils found in this period provides an important material for the study of the origin and evolution of human beings.

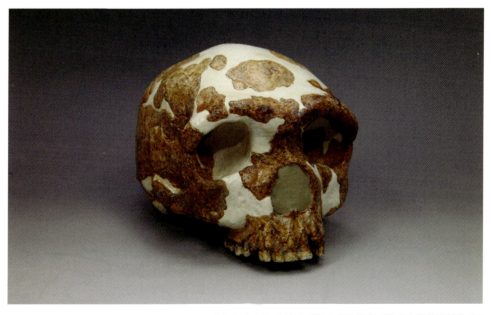

"金牛山人"头骨（藏于北京大学赛克勒考古与艺术博物馆）
Skull of Jinniushan Man (Arthur M. Sackler Museum of Art and Archaeology)

4.1.2 灰陶鸟形鬶

长岛位于胶东、辽东半岛之间，是山东省唯一的海岛县。位于长岛的北庄遗址面积 1 万平方米，遗址本身可分为几个不同的发展阶段。北大考古系在此先后进行了五次发掘。从北庄遗址出土的文物可以看出，早在 6000 年前胶、辽两地就有着海上交流。

这件灰陶鸟形鬶 1984 年出土于北庄遗址，高 19.3 厘米，长 23.5 厘米，属于大汶口文化北庄一期的遗存，手工制作，整体呈呼之欲飞、憨态可掬的鸟形。平背圆腹，三实足，流部为鸟头形，尾部上翘，塑造成为一个桶状的注水口。胶东地区的先民普遍把鸟视为其氏族的图腾，所以有许多器物的造型源自于鸟。这是其中较早的一件。

灰陶鸟形鬶（新石器时代晚期）（藏于北京大学赛克勒考古与艺术博物馆，编号：F64∶5）
Bird-shaped Grey Pottery Gui, Late Neolithic（Arthur M. Sackler Museum of Art and Archaeology, No. F64∶5）

4.1.2 Bird-shaped Grey Pottery Tripod

Long Island (Changdao Island) is located between Jiaodong and Liaodong peninsula. It is the only island county in Shandong Province. The Beizhuang site is about 10 000 square meters in size, which can be divided into several different stages of development. The Department of Archaeology (now the School of Archaeology and Museology), Peking University has carried out five excavations successively. According to the cultural relics unearthed from Beizhuang site, there were communications and exchanges over the sea between Jiaodong and Liaodong peninsula as early as 6000 years ago.

This bird shaped grey pottery Gui belongs to the Beizhuang I period, Dawenkou Culture. It was handmade and has the shape as a bird that is charmingly naive and is about to fly. It has flat back, oval-shape belly, and three solid legs. The head of the bird forms a spout while the bucket-shaped tail forms the water-filling nozzle. The ancestors of the Jiaodong area generally regarded the bird as the totem of their clan. Therefore, there are many artifacts derived from the image of bird. This is one of them from the earlier periods.

4.1.3 甲骨卜辞

北大赛克勒考古与艺术博物馆藏有字甲骨三千余片，原为1949年前北京大学与燕京大学购藏，皆为河南安阳殷墟出土。下图这片牛肩胛骨长32厘米，宽21厘米，高8厘米，其上是一篇包括叙辞、命辞、占辞及验辞的完整刻辞。字形工整，力度不凡。内容是卜问天象。卜辞大意是：己亥贞人㱿卜问次日庚子是否会下雨。王占断说：此卜预示庚子会下雨。结果是占卜当天（己亥）下雨了，次日庚子天空只出现了三色云，且很快就消失，天放晴了。

卜辞释文如下：己亥卜，㱿贞：翌庚子酚，其雨？王占曰：兹隹庚雨。卜之日雨。庚子酚，三䖒云，㸫其既。

甲骨卜辞商武丁时期（公元前13世纪）
Oracle inscription, 13th Century B.C.
（藏于北京大学赛克勒考古与艺术博物馆，编号：94.0420）
(Arthur M. Sackler Museum of Art and Archaeology. No. 94.0420)

4.1.3 Oracle Inscription

The Sackler Museum of Art and Archaeology in Peking University stores more than 3000 pieces of oracle bones with inscriptions. Originally bought by the former Peking University and Yenching University, these valuable oracle bones all were unearthed at Yinxu (Yin Ruins), Anyang city, Henan Province. This piece of ox scapula carries a complete inscription for the divination of Astronomical Phenomena. The characters are neat and orderly. The meaning of the inscription generally is : the diviner asked for whether if it would be a rainy day the next day. The king asserted that it showed that it would rain. At last, it turned out that it rained on the divination day. And on the day after that there were only three-color cloud appeared in the sky and they soon dispersed.

The inscriptions are as below: 己亥卜，㱿贞：翌庚子酓，其雨？王占曰：兹隹庚雨。卜之日雨。庚子酓，三䆈云，㽅其既。

4.1.4 叔虞方鼎

叔虞是周成王的弟弟，周成王即位之后，封叔虞到山西南部的唐，所以叔虞又被称为唐叔虞。这件鼎出土于叔虞的儿子燮父的墓中，是迄今我们所能看到的唯一一件唐叔虞的自制铜器，也为晋的始封地提供了确凿的证据。

叔虞方鼎（M114：217），器体方正，立耳，四角和每侧面中部都有扉棱。器身饰四组兽面纹，四圆柱足上饰焦叶纹。器内壁有 8 行 48 字的铭文。讲述了周历某年十四月，王在成周举行盛大祭典，并赏赐叔夨。叔夨称颂王的美德，铸鼎以志万年不忘。

鼎，山西省曲沃县曲村镇晋侯墓地 M114 出土（藏于北京大学赛克勒考古与艺术博物馆）
The Square-shaped Ding was Excavated from M114 of Marquis Jin (Jin Hou) Cemetery in Qucun Town, Quwo County, Shanxi Province. (Arthur M. Sackler Museum of Art and Archaeology)

4.1.4 Shuyu Square Ding

Shuyu was the younger brother of king Cheng of Zhou. After king Cheng came to the throne, he enfeoffed Shuyu to Tang which was in the south part of Shanxi Province. Therefore, Shuyu is also called Tang Shuyu. Unearthed from the tomb of Xiefu (Shuyu's son), this vessel is the only example of self-make bronze by Tang Shuyu so far we have. It also provides conclusive evidence for the original fief of Jin.

With two standing ears, Shuyu Square Ding (M114: 217) has a square and upright body. There are ridges on each four corners and also in the middle part of each side of this vessel. The body is decorated with four groups of animal faces; four cylindrical feet are ornamented with banana leaf pattern. There are 8 lines and 48 characters inscribed on the inner wall of this object. The inscription is about: in the fourteenth month of a certain year according to Zhou calendar, the King held a grand ceremony at Chengzhou, and rewarded Shuyu. Shuyu praised the King's virtues and casted this vessel to remember forever.

方鼎铭文：惟十又四月，王酓大褅，拜在成周。咸拜，王呼殷厥士，赏（赏）叔夨（虞）以裳、车马、贝卌朋。敢对王休，用作宝尊彝，其万年扬王光厥士。
The Inscriptions on Shuyu Square Ding

4.1.5 曲沃晋侯墓地 6214 号墓胸饰

这件华丽的胸佩饰是由一块梯形滑石板和其上侧穿缀一串、下侧穿缀十串玛瑙、绿松石、滑石贝、珠等组成的串饰构成。梯形滑石板的两面各刻有对称的双鸟，鸟的眼睛上镶嵌绿松石，做工精细。

晋侯墓出土了许多精美的西周玉器，为了解西周玉器提供了丰富可靠的资料。其玉器从使用功能上大致可分为礼仪、佩饰、丧葬用器。"将翱将翔，佩玉将将"，雍容华贵的佩饰衬托出女主人身份的显赫。

胸饰，山西省曲沃县曲村镇晋侯墓地第 6214 号墓出土（藏于北京大学赛克勒考古与艺术博物馆）
Breast Ornament from No. 6214 Burial of Marquis Jin, Qucun Town, Quwo County, Shanxi Province (Arthur M. Sackler Museum of Art and Archaeology.)

4.1.5 Breast Ornament

This spectacular and finely crafted breast ornament consists of a trapezoid-shaped talcum plague with one strung of beads on the upper side and ten strands of beads on the lower side. The strands are made of small tube-shaped beads and round beads of agate, turquoise, talc and pearls. The plague is carved with a symmetrical pair of birds whose eyes are inset with beads of turquoise.

A large number of jade objects of Zhou Dynasty were excavated from the burials of Marquis Jin that provide abundant and credible evidences to study the jade objects of West Zhou. According to their functions, these jade objects can be divided into ritual, decorative and funeral objects. "Like to fly, like to flitting, the jade ornaments she wears are tinkling". The lush and elegant accessories were about to demonstrate their prominent hostess.

4.1.6 佉卢文刻石

1924年北大马衡在洛阳发现并带回了三块佉卢文残石,这块佉卢文刻石是其中之一,属于佛教寺院中的井栏。佉卢文最早起源于古代犍陀罗地区,是公元前3世纪印度孔雀王朝阿育王时期的文字,早期在印度西北部和今巴基斯坦一带使用,公元1—2世纪时在中亚地区广泛传播。

这件井栏上佉卢文的大意是:某年某月第十五日,祈愿四方僧团的僧人受到敬重。佛教在中国社会产生了广泛而深刻的影响,佛教传入中国的时间学术界有不同的看法,这件佉卢文残石证明东汉末年,都城洛阳有外国僧团的活动。

刻石(藏于北京大学赛克勒考古与艺术博物馆,编号:95.4224/37.1.375-1)
Carving Stone (Arthur M. Sackler Museum of Art and Archaeology, No. 95.4224/37.1.375-1)

4.1.6 Carving Stone with Kharosthi Script

This is one of the three pieces of carving stones with Kharosthi Script discovered in Luoyang by Ma Heng of Peking University in 1924. It was part of the well curb in a Buddhist temple. Originated in the ancient Gandhara area, the Kharosthi was used during the Ashoka period of the Maurya Dynasty (about 3rd Century BC). It was used at the earliest in the areas of northwest India and Pakistan, and then widely spread in Central Asia during the $1^{st} – 2^{nd}$ Century.

The content of this piece is about: on the fifteenth day of a certain month in a certain year, the monks from the "Monastic order invocating for all sides" were respected. Buddhism has profound influence on Chinese society. However, scholars have different views about the concrete time when Buddhism came to China. This piece of stone with Kharosthi Script proves that during the Eastern Han Dynasty there was a foreign sangha in Luoyang, the capital of China at that time.

4.1.7 八曲铜镜

八曲铜镜为唐代文物,直径 15.2 厘米。镜子有一龟钮。背面浮雕纹饰,表现的是神仙人物故事。

上方为流云、山峦和半月,铸有"侯谨之"。左面的竹林下端坐一人,双膝间置琴,前置几,上有笔砚。右侧有起舞的凤鸟,下方的水池中露出荷叶。同类的铜镜有名"真子飞霜"者,所以这类铜镜一般被称为"真子飞霜"镜,也有学者称为"伯牙弹琴镜"。

八曲铜镜(唐代)(藏于北京大学赛克勒考古与艺术博物馆,编号:1932.21)
Mirror with Scalloped Edges, Tang Dynasty (Arthur M. Sackler Museum of Art and Archaeology, No. 1932.21)

4.1.7 Mirror with Scalloped Edges

This mirror has a tortoise-shaped Knob. And the back of this mirror is covered with designs sculpted in relief to show the immortal characters.

In the upper portion there are clouds, mountains, and a half moon together with a three-character inscription "*Hou Jinzhi*". On the left hand side there is a strand of bamboo and a man sitting up straight with a Qin, a traditional string instrument in China, between his legs. Placed before him is a small table on top of which rests a calligraphy brush, an ink stone, and other writing tools. On the right hand side of the mirror there is a dancing Phoenix. Below is a small pond out of which grows a tall lotus leaf. Among mirrors similar to this one in shape and decoration, some bear the inscription "*Zhen zi fei shuang*" (the meaning is unclear). Because of this, mirrors like this are commonly referred to as "*Zhen zi fei shuang*" mirrors. However, there are also some scholars who refers this mirror as "Boya Playing the Qin" mirrors, which is about the story of a famous Spring and Autumn Period qin player.

4.1.8 景德镇窑卵白釉"太禧"瓷盘

景德镇窑卵白釉"太禧"瓷盘为元代后期文物，高 3.4 厘米，口径 17.8 厘米，底径 11.4 厘米。瓷盘圆唇、敞口、矮圈足。盘心印龙戏珠纹。内壁腹部印缠枝莲花，上托八宝，纹饰间对称印"太禧"二字。

卵白釉瓷器中带"枢府"（枢密院）款的较多，带"太禧"款的绝少。

卵白釉是元代景德镇窑新创烧的一种高温釉，因釉色似鹅蛋，呈现白中微泛青的色调而得名。瓷器的装饰以印花为主，纹饰题材以云龙和缠枝花卉纹为常见。制作精细的缠枝花卉纹样中常有"枢府""太禧""福禄"等铭文。"太禧"太禧宗禋院（元朝专掌朝廷祭祀机构）定制的用瓷。

景德镇窑卵白釉"太禧"瓷盘（藏于北京大学赛克勒考古与艺术博物馆，编号：96.0333/1949.54）
Eggshell White Glaze Porcelain with Inscription of "Tai Xi", Jingdezhen Kiln (Arthur M. Sackler Museum of Art and Archaeology, No. 96.0333/1949.54)

4.1.8 Eggshell White Glaze Porcelain with Inscription of "Tai Xi", Jingdezhen Kiln

This plate has round lip, open-top, and short ring foot. It is decorated with a pattern of dragons playing a ball in the middle and interlocking lotus raising eight treasures in the inner wall of the abdomen of the plate. There are symmetric two characters "Tai Xi" among all these decorations.

There are a few examples of eggshell white glazed porcelain with "Shu Fu" (the Privy Council) inscription while it is more rarely of them with "Tai Xi" inscription.

Eggshell white glaze is a kind of high temperature glaze created by Jingdezhen kiln during Yuan Dynasty. It got the name because the glaze has similar appearance of the color of goose egg. Eggshell white glaze porcelains were mostly decorated with printing. Cloud dragon and interlocking floral are the most common designs. There always are characters of "Shu Fu" "Tai Xi", and "Fu Lu"(happiness and affluence) among elaborated interlocking floral patterns. "Tai Xi" illustrates that these objects were specially made for the Tai Xi Zong Yin Yuan, which was the department of sacrifice ceremonies for royal or imperial court in Yuan Dynasty.

4.2 古籍善本
4.2 Chinese Rare Book Collection

4.2.1 西汉竹书《老子》

2009年1月，北大赛克勒考古与艺术博物馆入藏了一批珍贵的西汉竹书，共有3364枚竹简，包括了小学、史书、子书、小说、数术和医方等。据字形和书体特征判断，抄写年代大概在汉武帝晚期到汉宣帝之间，其中就有这部《老子》，这是继郭店楚简本和西汉马王堆汉墓帛书甲乙本之后的又一个重要的《老子》版本，有接近完整的竹简211枚，残简10枚，5200多字，分为77章，很完整地保存了《老子》的篇章结构和文字。竹简背后还题有"老子上经""老子下经"两个篇题，分别对应《德经》和《道经》，这也是《老子》书名在简帛文献中的首次发现，证实了《老子》称"经"的古代文献记载。这部文献为研究道家经典《老子》的早期文本演变和秦汉时期文书学的发展提供了难以取代的资料。

竹简
Bamboo Slips

Chapter Four: Safeguard of Civilization
第四章　文明的守护

4.2.1 Western Han Bamboo Manuscript of the *Laozi*

In January 2009, the Sackler Museum of Peking University accepted a precious collection of Western Han (202BC – 8) bamboo scripts, including texts of elementary learning, anecdotes, history, ancient masters, the mantic arts, and medical texts. Judging from the style of the scripts, these texts were copied between the reigns of Emperor Wu (r.141 – 87BC) and Emperor Xuan (r.74 – 48BC) of the Western Han. Among these texts is this manuscript of the *Laozi*, which is another important early copy of this work following the unearthed bamboo manuscript from Guodian and the silk manuscript from Mawangdui. It contains 211 nearly intact bamboo slips and 10 fragmented ones, with the remaining 5200 characters divided into 77 chapters, and preserves nicely the structure and writing of this text. On the back of the bamboo slips appear the titles of "Upper Jing of the *Laozi*" and "Lower Jing of the *Laozi*," corresponding in turn to *De Jing* and *Dao Jing*. This is also the first time the title Laozi has been found in early bamboo and silk manuscripts. It confirms the historical account that the *Laozi* was referred as the *Jing* (scripture). This manuscript thus provides important clues to the development of the text of the *Laozi* as well as manuscript culture during the Qin and Han periods.

竹简
Bamboo Slips

4.2.2 西汉竹书《妄稽》

在中国早期文学体裁里,赋是极有代表性的一种。北大收藏的西汉竹书里,就有一篇奇特而饶有趣味的俗赋,题为《妄稽》,有完整简 73 枚,残简 15 枚,所存文字约 2700 字,全文基本是四言并且隔句为韵,也有连续几句押韵。比起尹湾汉墓出土的著名俗赋《神乌赋》,篇幅要大得多,但性质上和《神乌赋》类似,也是叙事体。全文讲述西汉时荥阳一位叫周春的男子,性情温和,相貌"美好姱丽",却娶了一位"甚丑以恶"的妻子妄稽。周春厌恶妄稽到"日夜流涕"的地步,并遍告乡党。他父母于是为他买来"靡曼白皙,长发诱绐"的美妾虞士。但妄稽是出名的妒妇,于是嫉恨到"昏笞虞士,至旦不已"的地步,软弱的周春虽爱虞士,竟无能为力。后来妄稽生了大病,临死前对自己的妒行表示深深反悔,将家财都送给虞士。《妄稽》全文诙谐而夸张,文辞也铺陈华丽,作者也许有宣扬家庭道德训诫的目的,但能不受拘束地描摹当时日常中的人情世故,在早期文学中甚为罕见。

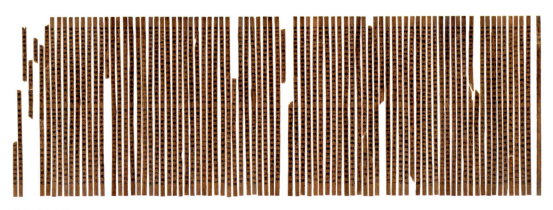

竹书《妄稽》
Bamboo Manuscript of the *Wangji*

4.2.2 Western Han Bamboo Manuscript of the *Wangji*

Fu (rhymed prose) was a major genre in the early Chinese literary tradition. Among the Sackler Museum's collection of Western Han (202BC – 8) bamboo manuscripts is a unique and interesting vernacular *fu* titled the *Wangji* (literally, "Presumptuous Accusation"). It contains 73 nearly intact bamboo slips and 15 fragmented ones, and 2700 characters, and is composed of four-character lines with rhymes in every other line or sometimes consecutive rhymes. Compared with the famous vernacular *fu* poetry of the *Shenniao Fu* (Fu of the Divine Bird) unearthed in the Han tomb of Yinwan, the *Wangji* is similar in nature by adopting a narrative structure, but much expanded in its scope. It tells the story of a gentle and handsome Western Han man named Zhou Chun, who lived in Xingyang and married an ugly and devious woman named Wangji. He loathed her so much that he shed tears day and night and told all his relatives about his feelings. His parents therefore brought him a slender and white-skinned concubine, Lady Yu, with long hair. His jealous wife Wangji, however, was so infuriated that she tortured Lady Yu day and night, but Zhou Chun was too timid to do anything to intervene. Shortly afterward Wangji became seriously ill, and on the eve of her death she showed remorse for her jealousy and handed over all her possessions to Lady Yu. The text of the *Wangji* is humorous and has an elaborate, flamboyant writing style. while the purpose of composing such piece might have been didactic, yet the writing provides a rather unbridled depiction human emotions and daily life, which is rare in early Chinese literature.

Bamboo Manuscript

4.2.3 吐鲁番文书《北凉承平年间写高昌赀簿》

藏于北大图书馆的这一纸质残片,从形状判断是古人用书写过的废弃纸张剪贴而成的一个鞋帮。这件看起来很不起眼的东西,其实是一份意义重大的历史资料。残片正反面的书写带有浓厚"波磔"状隶意,记录的都是十六国时期北凉统治下高昌地区的计赀制度,也就是当地政权按照民户的土地等财产的多少来确定税收额度,所以被研究者定名为"赀簿"。这不仅是吐鲁番地区出土的古代文书中时间最早的一种,而且为人们了解丝绸之路上重要的中心——高昌在中古早期的经济生活提供了第一手资料。这一文献很可能是出土于吐鲁番胜金口的北凉时期高昌赀簿文书残片之一,并为清末长期在新疆任官的著名学者王树枏所得。王树枏后来将这些残片带到北京出售,其中一部分最终进入了北大图书馆。

《北凉承平年间写高昌赀簿》残片
Paper Fragment of *Property Registration Record of the Kingdom of Gaochang*

4.2.3 *Property Registration Record of the Kingdom of Gaochang*

An ancient paper fragment in the shape of the upper part of a shoe is in the Peking University Library collection. Yet this seemingly inconspicuous piece of paper, apparently reused by ancient people, is in fact a significant historical document from ancient Turfan. The scripts on both sides of the paper are in the style of a tilted stroke, and the text, which dates to the Chengping era of the Northern Liang, records information on household properties in the Gaochang area under the Northern Liang (397 or 401 – 439). Such records formed the basis of taxation by the local administration of Gaochang. Not only is this one of the earliest surviving ancient documents from Turfan, but it also provides invaluable information on the economic life of ancient Gaochang, which was a major center of the ancient Silk Road. This fragment may very well have belonged to those documents of Turfan discovered in Shengjingkou, and entered the collection of the famous scholar Wang Shunan, who served as an administrator in Xinjiang in the late Qing. Later Wang brought these documents to Beijing for sale, some of which eventually ended up in the University library.

4.2.4 唐写本《妙法莲华经观世音菩萨普门品》

　　《妙法莲华经》是古代印度最为重要的大乘佛教经典之一。在中国中古时代，该经数度被译成汉文，而由来自龟兹的高僧鸠摩罗什主持的译本，因意旨精确、文辞典雅而流行最广、影响最大。罗什译本《法华经》第二十五品是《观世音普门品》，更是在《法华经》本身流行的基础上为当时广受民众追随的观音崇拜提供了文本依据，于是往往被信众视为《观音经》而单独抄写弘扬。北大所藏的这部写本出自敦煌遗书。根据写本题记，这是武周天授二年（691年）九月三十日佛教信徒令狐兰为功德而出资制作，书人为张晋朝。题记中不仅有令狐兰的愿文，也有张晋朝的祈愿。启功先生评价此卷"书体清劲"，有"六朝遗韵"，是写经书法的"上品"。加上有可靠纪年，为了解唐前期流行书体提供了珍贵信息。

《妙法莲华经观世音菩萨普门品》
Sutra of the Lotus of the Wonderful Law

4.2.4 The *Sutra of the Lotus of the Wonderful Law,* Manuscript from Dunhuang

The *Sutra of the Lotus of the Wonderful Law* (*Miao fa lian hua jing*, Skt. *Saddharmapuṇḍarīka-sūtra*), commonly known as the Lotus Sutra, is one of the most influential Buddhist scriptures in the Indian Mahayana tradition. In medieval China, the text was translated into Chinese several times, but the most popular version remains the translation made under the supervision of the famous Kucharian master Kumārajiva for its accurate and refined language. The twenty-fifth chapter of Kumārajiva's translation is titled "The Bodhisattva Avalokiteśvara's Gateway to Every Direction" (*Guan shi yin pu men pin*). It further provided the canonical foundation for the popular worship of Bodhisattva Avalokiteśvara (*Guan shi yin*) in medieval China. This chapter was often copied alone by pious followers of the Buddhist teaching. This scroll from the Peking University collection once belonged to the manuscripts discovered in Dunhuang in the early 20th century. According to the colophon of the scroll, it was commissioned by Linghu Lan as a devotional act and copied by calligrapher Zhang Jinchao on the 30th day of the ninth month of the second year of Tianshou (691) during the time of Empress Wu (r.690 – 705). It is rare among this type of sutra copies to have a colophon that records not only an accurate date, but also the prayer of both the sponsor and the copier. Qi Gong (1912 – 2005), one of the foremost scholars of Chinese calligraphy, considers this piece a supreme example of Buddhist calligraphy of medieval China.

4.2.5 南宋天香书院刻本《监本纂图重言重意互注论语》

　　《论语》为儒家经典十三经中的一种，记载孔子及孔门弟子言行，集中体现了孔子的道德理想和政治主张。三国魏正始中，何晏等人汇集前代诸家有关《论语》的注释，编为《论语集解》十卷，成为后世通行的《论语》文本。宋代多见《论语集解》刊刻的记载，但今日流传极为罕见，北京大学图书馆所藏宋刻《监本纂图重言重意互注论语》二卷，是今日仅存的宋刻《论语集解》经注本。此本将《论语集解》原十卷改编为二卷，卷前刻"鲁国城里之图"一幅，行间刻句读，并增入便于理解记忆的重言、重意、互注等内容。这些辅助方法都是为了让此书更便于参加科举的士子学习，可以说是当时科举文化和发达的商业出版结合的例证。此本有牌记"刘氏天香书院之记"。纸墨精雅，刻印俱佳。从内容、版刻风格看，此本当为南宋福建地区的刻本。原藏日本，清末学者杨守敬以重金购得，后辗转归李盛铎所有。书中有杨守敬、袁克文跋文，称此本"为自来著录家所不及"，"为南宋绝精之刻"。

Chapter Four: Safeguard of Civilization
第四章 文明的守护

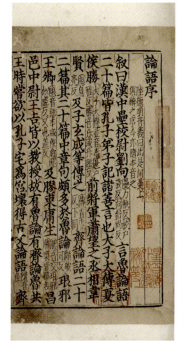 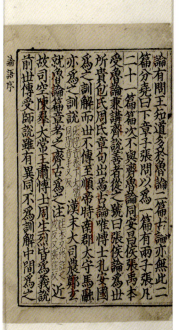 

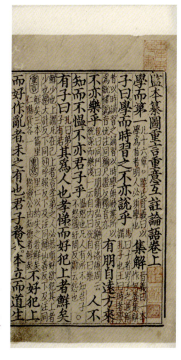 

南宋天香书院刻本《监本纂图重言重意互注论语》
Heavenly Fragrance Book House–Printed Edition of the *Analects*, Southern Song

4.2.5 Heavenly Fragrance Book House–Printed Edition of the *Analects*, Southern Song

The *Analects* (*Lun yu*), one of the 13 Classics in the Confucian canon, records the words and actions of Kong Zi (i.e., Confucius, 551 – 479 BC) and his disciples, and has been considered the most authoritative source for learning Kong Zi's moral principles and political ideology. During the Zhengshi era (240 – 249) of the Wei Dynasty (220 – 266), He Yan (195? – 249) assembled the extant commentaries on the Analects and put together the *Collected Commentaries of the Analects* (*Lun yu Ji jie*) in 10 juan, which became the standard edition of the Analects circulated in later centuries. Song era (960 – 1279) sources provide a great deal of information about the publication of this text. The copy possessed by the University library is the sole surviving Song-printed copy today. The full title of this text is *Jianben Zuantu Chongyan Chongyi Huzhu Lunyu*, which translates literally as *Imperial Academy Edition of the Analects with Compiled Illustrations, Notation of Repeating Phrases and Repeating Meaning, and Inter-textual Commentaries*. This edition reorganized the original 10 juan *Collected Commentaries* into a two juan work. At the beginning of the text is an illustrated "Map of the Towns of the State of Lu." The text itself is punctuated, and also applies the so-called "notation of repeating phrases" (*chong yan*), meaning that it indicates how many times the same phrase appears throughout the entire text, and the "notation of repeating meaning"(*chong yi*), meaning that the text points out phrases with similar meaning in different sections of the Analects. "Inter-textual commentaries"(*hu zhu*) means that this edition quotes phrases from other Confucian Classics to explain the meaning of certain phrases in the *Analects*. These methods were commonly employed by commercial book sellers to make the Confucian Classics easier for examination candidates to study and check. This copy is thus a telling example of the mutual support of Song examination culture and advanced printing culture. The book, with exceptional-quality engravings, ink color, and paper, was the product of a commercial printing shop called the Heavenly Fragrance Book House of the Liu Family (*Liu shi tian xiang shu yuan*). Judging from its content and stylistic features, it must have come from the Fujian area during the

Southern Song. Originally kept in Japan, it was later acquired by Yang Shoujing (1839 – 1915) and eventually went to Li Shengduo (1859 – 1937) before coming to the University library. Eminent rare book collectors and connoisseurs such as Yang Shoujing and Yuan Kewen (1889 – 1931) considered this copy one of the finest examples of books produced by woodblock printing in the Southern Song.

4.2.6 南宋黄善夫刻本《汉书》《后汉书》

南宋时期我国雕版印刷技术空前发展，形成了几个大的刻书中心，其中以福建建阳地区民间刻书最为兴盛，世称"建本"，福建建安人黄善夫即是建阳地区著名的刻书者，所刻"三史"刻印精美，被称为"建本"代表作。"三史"包括《史记》《汉书》与《后汉书》，是我国纪传体史书"二十四史"中最早也最重要的三部著作。黄善夫刊刻"三史"的时间约在光宗绍熙至宁宗庆元间，其行款字数与刊刻风格一致，堪称一套样式统一的"丛书"。书板刻成后曾经转手，故有初印与改版后印之别。黄善夫本"三史"传世皆极稀少，且多残本，北京大学图书馆有幸藏有其中的两部全本，蔚为大观。其中《汉书》一百卷，东汉班固撰，有"建安黄善夫刊于家塾之敬室"牌记，又有改刻"建安刘元起刊于家塾之敬室"牌记，为修版后印本。《后汉书》一百二十卷，南朝宋范晔撰，有"建安黄善夫刊于家塾之敬室"牌记，为初印本。二本皆刻工精湛，楮墨莹洁，为我国雕版印刷史名品。

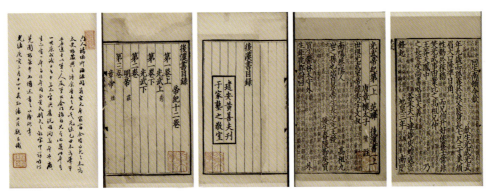

《后汉书》
Hou Hanshu

4.2.6 Southern Song Printed Editions of the *Hanshu* and *Hou Hanshu*

The Southern Song witnessed the formation of a highly advanced and competitive woodblock printing industry. This industry had several regional centers, one of which was in Jianyang in Fujian, and those texts published in Southern Song Jianyang are referred to as a "*Jian* edition." Among the finest examples of a *Jian* edition are the Three Histories—namely, the *Shi ji* (Records of the Grand Scribe), *Hanshu* (History of the Han), and *Hou Han shu* (History of the Later Han)—published by the workshop of Huang Shanfu, a native of Jian'an from Fujian and famous publisher in Jianyang. These are also the three earliest and most important historiographies of the so-called Twenty-four Dynastic Histories (*Er shi si shi*). The Huang Shanfu edition of the Three Histories was printed between the Shaoxi era (1190 – 1194) and the Qingyuan era (1195 – 1200). All three are stylistically consistent and have the same page layout, making them appear more like a book series. The woodblocks used for the printing changed hands after the initial print, resulting in differences between that and later printings. Although most surviving copies of the Three Histories printed by Huang Shanfu are incomplete and fragmentary, the copies of the *Hanshu* and *Hou Hanshu* in the University collection are complete and thus extremely rare. The copy of the *Hanshu*, in 100 juan, mentions Huang Shanfu and Liu Yuanqi as the publishers, indicating that it was printed by Liu Yuanqi's workshop using retouched woodblocks from Huang Shanfu's workshop. Meanwhile, the copy of the *Hou Hanshu*, in 120 juan, was printed from the original woodblocks of Huang's workshop.

4.2.7 宋刻《攻媿先生文集》

楼钥（1137—1213）字大防，又字启伯，南宋时明州鄞县（今浙江宁波）人。他是南宋重要文人官僚，自宋孝宗隆兴元年（1163年）进士及第后，即进入了漫长而成功的仕途。大定九年（1169年），他以书状官身份从舅父汪大猷出使金朝，按日记叙途中所闻，撰成著名的《北行日录》，这是有关金朝情形的珍贵记录。楼钥很早就以文辞和学识闻名，因此长时间在朝廷负责文书工作，这也使他得以参与南宋的中枢政治。宁宗即位之初，他在政治上支持赵汝愚，反对权臣韩侂胄，并为受到政治迫害的朱熹鸣不平。庆元党禁后，他辞官居家十三年。等韩侂胄被诛，才重新回到朝廷担任参知政事等职位。楼钥著述丰富，诗文在南宋朝野士大夫中很有影响，为南宋朝廷的"大手笔"之一。他以攻媿名斋，故号攻媿主人。北大所藏的这部《攻媿先生文集》，是南宋四明楼氏家出品，雕印俱佳，是南宋后期浙东刻书之范例。因其字体秀丽匀称，在"文革"后期被用于印刷线装版毛泽东诗词。此刻本包括诗文一百二十卷和目录五卷，是现存最早也是最为完备的楼钥诗文集。

《攻媿先生文集》
Collected Works of Lou Yue

4.2.7 Southern Song Edition of the *Collected Works of Lou Yue*, 120 juan, with catalogue, 5 juan

The Southern Song scholar-official Lou Yue (1137 – 1213) was a native of Ningbo whose long and illustrious official career started shortly after he passed the Jinshi examination in 1163. In 1169, he was dispatched by the Southern Song court as a secretary to accompany his uncle Wang Dayou for a diplomatic mission to the Jurchen Jin Dynasty. His account of the social and political situation of the Jurchen, who ruled Northern China, resulted in the valuable *Bei xing ri lu* (Daily Record of the Northern Journey). Known since his early career for his learning and literary skills, Lou Yue's long involvement in the business of drafting court documents also put him at the center of Southern Song court politics. He was a prolific writer whose prose and poetry were greatly admired among the Southern Song educated elite, and he was considered one of the literary luminaries of his time. This woodblock print of the *Collected Works of Lou Yue* was a production of the printing shop of the Lou Family of Siming. Its exceptionally high quality makes it a fine example of printing culture of the Eastern Zhejiang during the later Southern Song. This is also the most complete extant edition of Lou Yue's works. The elegant and well-proportioned script of this printed edition was selected during the "Cultural Revolution" as the script for the woodblock printing of Mao Zedong's collected poetry.

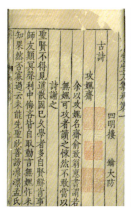

《攻媿先生文集》
Collected Works of Lou Yue

4.2.8 南宋刻本《五曹算经》

《五曹算经》被认为是唐李淳风等编写的算术书。所谓五曹，即田、兵、集、仓、金曹。这些都是中古以来地方行政系统中负责财赋管理和人员调动的部门，《五曹算经》正是从那些部门的实际需要出发来编写的，里面的 67 道算术题涉及的是各曹常见的事项。形式是先提出问题，随后提供答案，接下来再作解释。比如仓曹部分有题如下：

> 今有粟七百斛，欲雇车运之，每一斛雇七升。问车主、粟主各几何？
> 答曰：车主四十九斛；粟主六百五十一斛。
> 术曰：列粟七百斛，以雇粟七升乘之，得四十九斛，为车粟。以减本粟七百斛，余为主粟。

北大图书馆保存的这部南宋刻本，是现存《五曹算经》的孤帙。嘉定六年（1213年），任官于福建汀州的天文数学家鲍澣之根据北宋元丰监本，刊刻了包括《五曹算经》在内的重要算书。这也是世界上现存最早的印刷本算学课本之一。

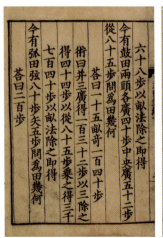 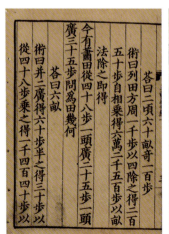 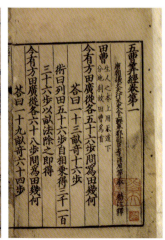

《五曹算经》
Classic of Arithmetic of the Five Bureaus

4.2.8 Southern Song Edition of the *Classic of Arithmetic of the Five Bureaus*

The compilation of the *Classic of Arithmetic of the Five Bureaus* (*Wu cao suan jing*) has been attributed to the Tang Dynasty astronomer Li Chunfeng (602 – 670). The five bureaus appearing in the title of the text refer to the five sections of local administration that were responsible for financial and personnel management from medieval China onward, namely, the bureaus of land, military service, accounts, granaries, and revenue. This text was put together for the practical needs of these government offices, and the 67 arithmetic problems included in this text reflect common issues they dealt with. For example, a typical problem from the bureau of granaries was the following:

One has 700 hu of millet, and needs to hire a cart owner to transport them. He has to pay the cart owner 7 sheng (1 sheng is approximately 1/49 hu) out of each hu. How many hu will the millet owner and the cart owner receive at the end?

Answer: The cart owner receives 49 hu, and the millet owner receives 651 hu.

Method: 700 hu times 7 sheng is 49 hu; this is the portion the cart owner receives. That deducting 49 hu from 700 is the portion the millet owner receives.

This Southern Song printed edition is the only extant copy of this text, and is also one of the earliest extant copies of textbooks of arithmetic in the world. It was printed in 1213 by the astronomer and mathematician Bao Wuzhi when he served in the local government in Fujian. This edition, based on the edition of the Northern Song imperial academy, was among several important mathematical treatises printed by Bao.

4.2.9 元刻《宋提刑洗冤集录》

宋代是帝制中国司法流程和刑事侦讯手段日趋成熟完备的时代。北大所藏的这一部元刻《宋提刑洗冤集录》可以说是这方面的重要代表。此书是世上现存最早的法医学著作，宋提刑是指作者宋慈（1186—1249），他是南宋时人，深受朱熹理学影响，进士及第后有丰富的地方任官经历，曾任广东和湖南等地的提点刑狱，在法医学方面积累了宝贵经验。淳祐七年（1247年），在湖南提点刑狱任上的宋慈综合了当时法医知识和本人经验，编成这部著作。全书五卷五十三目，从验尸官应该遵循的条令和准则，到法医检验中遇到的重要问题，比如暴力还是非暴力死亡、伤口的性质、尸体现象等都有精细的讨论。他特别强调司法中判定死者"幽枉屈伸"之关系重大，因此刑官一定要做到不辞辛劳，亲自调查。现代研究者认为书中提供的法医知识很多符合现代科学原理，比如"被打勒死假作自缢"一条说如果死后被人用绳索系扎手脚及头颈下等处，因为人已死，血气不行，所以"痕无血荫""虽被系缚深入皮，无青紫赤色，但只是白痕。"又提到用类似人工呼吸法救自缢者，用酸来沉淀和保护伤口等。该著作的论述体现出南宋法医方法的先进。这部著作自宋以后一直被视为法医学的经典，晚清以来更被译成多种欧洲文字。北大藏本则是现存此著最早的版本。

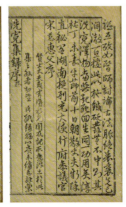
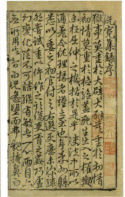

《宋提刑洗冤集录》
Collected Records of Washed Grievances of Judicial Commissioner Song

4.2.9 The Yuan Edition of the *Collected Records of Washed Grievances of Judicial Commissioner Song*

The Song Dynasty was an age of growing sophistication in judicial procedure and crime investigation in imperial China. The *Collected Records of Washed Grievances of Judicial Commissioner Song* (*Song tixing xi yuan ji lu*) is a good example of this development. The earliest extant forensic study in the world, its author was Southern Song (1127 – 1279) official Song Ci (1186 – 1249). Deeply influenced by Zhu Xi's Neo-Confucianism, Song Ci had extensive experience in forensic technique as a local judicial official in Guangdong and Hunan. In 1247, while serving as judicial commissioner of Hunan, he put together this text based on his own experience and the forensic knowledge available at the time. The entire work, containing 5 juan, consists of 53 categories, ranging from the regulations and principles for the coroner to follow to frequently encountered forensic problems, such as cause of death, the nature of wounds, and various phenomena associated with the corpse. Song Ci stressed the importance of forensic investigation throughout the entire judicial process for its role in serving justice for the dead. Many opinions in the discussions on forensic problems are supported by modern science. This work demonstrates the advancement of forensic medicine in the Southern Song, and it remained a classic in this field for many centuries afterward. It has also been translated into several Western languages since the late Qing. This Yuan (1271 – 1368) edition in the University collection is the earliest extant copy of the work.

4.2.10 元修明刻《新编金匮方论》

北大珍藏了多部古代重要医典的世间孤本,其中之一是这部元刻《新编金匮方论》。《新编金匮方论》即《金匮要略》,书的内容可追溯到汉代医圣张仲景的医典《伤寒杂病论》。《伤寒杂病论》中论杂病的部分汉以后散佚,直到北宋时翰林学士王洙在宫廷书库里找到了一部三卷本的《金匮玉函要略方》,才发现其中有那部分内容。该书上卷讲伤寒,中卷讲杂病,下卷载方剂及治疗妇科病。神宗熙宁时,朝廷召集医局儒臣孙奇、林亿等人校订此书,林亿等去掉了与当时流行的《伤寒论》内容重复的部分,保留杂病以下部分,并用他书中仲景方补填缺佚部分,这样重编后成了《金匮要略》,其大字本刊行于治平三年(1066年)。北大所藏本子系元·后至元六年(1340年)一位叫邓珍的福建人士获得大字本后将之重刊的版本,明嘉靖间又修刻重印。这是现存最早的本子,曾经清末著名学者杨守敬、李盛铎等收藏。不过准确指出这一刻本重要文献学价值的是日本医学史家真柳诚。真柳诚20世纪80年代时曾留学北大,注意到了此书的价值,他的看法不久获得了中日学界的赞同。

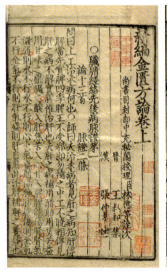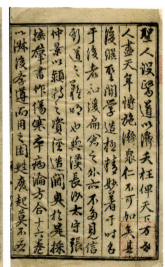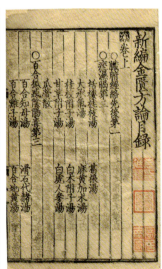

《新编金匮方论》
Newly Compiled Treatise on Medicinal Recipes from the Golden Coffer

4.2.10 *Newly Compiled Treatise on Medicinal Recipes from the Golden Coffer*

The *Xin bian jin gui fang lun*, which translates literally as *Newly Compiled Treatise on Medicinal Prescriptions of the Golden Coffer*, was printed with revisions during the Jiajing era (1522 – 1566) of the Ming based on a Yuan period woodblock edition. It is among a number of rare editions of important ancient medical texts collected by the University library. The content of this work is said to be related to the medical classic *Treatise on Cold Pathogenic and Miscellaneous Diseases* (*Shang han za bing lun*) compiled by the eminent Eastern Han (25 – 220) physician Zhang Zhongjing (150 – 219). The section on miscellaneous diseases in Zhang's text was believed lost after the Han until the Northern Song (960 – 1127) Hanlin Academician Wang Zhu(997 – 1057) discovered its contents in a medical compendium called *Essential Prescriptions of the Golden Coffer and Jade Casket* (*Jing gui yu han yao lue fang*) from the imperial library. During the Xining era (1068 – 1077) of Emperor Shenzong (r.1067 – 1085), under the command of the court, members of the Imperial Bureau of Medicine such as Sun Qi and Lin Yi re-edited this text and published a new edition with large script in 1066. The copy kept by the University library is a Ming Dynasty revised edition based on the version printed by Deng Zhen in 1340 after the latter obtained a copy of the 1066 edition. This is the earliest extant copy of the text and was once possessed by famous book collectors like Yang Shoujing (1839 – 1915) and Li Shengduo (1859 – 1937) in modern times. But the first scholar to point out correctly its textual value was Japanese scholar Mayanagi Makoto, who studied at Peking University in 1980s. His views on this matter are now widely accepted by scholars in the field of history of medicine.

4.2.11 元刻明印本《无锡志》

　　北大图书馆藏有许多珍贵的地方志，其中元刻明初印本元代王仁辅的《无锡志》是著名的一种。无锡历史十分悠久，宋代以来更成为四方商贾辐辏的江南名邑，但是元以前关于无锡的地方志都已佚失，这部《无锡志》是关于该地的现存最早的志书，而北大的版本又是最早的本子。该书作者王仁辅是元代文士，与大画家倪瓒关系密切，被后者尊奉为师。仁辅长年侨居无锡，对当地风土了若指掌，在至正年间编成《无锡志》。全书原为 28 卷，后编为 4 卷，分为 21 目，介绍无锡的山川地理、行政沿革、人文历史和历代诗文。但此书元代之后流传不广，直到清乾隆时编《四库全书》时才重新引起四库馆臣的注意，被认为是"词简而事赅"的地志善本，从而成为收入四库的极少数地志之一。此本原藏清代翰林院，清末流入李盛铎家，与李氏木犀轩其他善本一起归入北大。

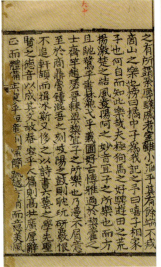 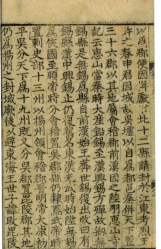 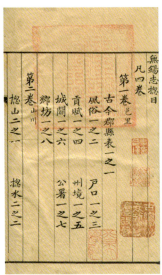

《无锡志》
Gazetteer of Wuxi

4.2.11 The *Gazetteer of Wuxi*

This copy of the *Gazetteer of Wuxi* (*Wuxi zhi*), compiled by Yuan Dynasty (1271 – 1368) scholar Wang Renfu, is among a great number of precious local gazetteers collected by the University. It was printed in the early Ming using Yuan woodblocks. Wuxi became one of the richest and most vibrant towns in the Jiangnan region from the time of the Song. Yet the local gazetteers of Wuxi produced before the Yuan era were all lost. This one by Wang Renfu is the earliest extant record of this locality, while the Peking University copy is the earliest surviving copy of this text. As a literatus, Wang Renfu befriended such great artists as Ni Zan (1301 – 1374), who considered Wang Renfu his mentor. A long-time resident of Wuxi, Wang Renfu compiled this gazetteer during the Zhizheng era of the Yuan. The entire book initially had 28 juan but was later reorganized into four juan and 21 sections. It introduced geography, the historical changes of administrative units, the culture and history of the area, and notable literary works dedicated to famous sites. Circulation of the *Gazetteer of Wuxi* remained limited after the Yuan era until compilers of the imperial-sanctioned *Complete Library of the Four Treasures in Qing* took note of it. Considering this text one of the finest examples of local gazetteers in its scholarly quality, they included it in the *Complete Library*. This copy was originally kept in the Hanlin Academy during the Qing and entered the personal collection of Li Shengduo (1859 – 1937) toward the end of the dynasty. This book, along with many other rare books from Li's collection, was eventually sold to Peking University.

4.2.12 明万历年间刻五色套印本《十竹斋书画谱》

十竹斋是明末画家胡正言在南京的斋名,也是他的工作坊。《十竹斋书画谱》就是他主持辑印的一套供人学习绘画笔法构图的教材。这套画谱分书画、墨华、果、翎毛、兰、竹谱、梅、石八大类,每一类都有当时名人作序题字。画谱中刊印的除了胡正言自己的画作,还有当时名家的作品,在提供绘画样本的同时还教授作画步骤。这套画谱先将画稿的不同颜色分别勾摹下来,然后镌刻在称为"饾版"的小木板上,通过套印和叠印技术,不仅能完整地将原画中的色彩印制出来,还能用水印细腻地表现出笔墨晕染的浓淡深浅,和原作几乎无差。这是中国版刻史上的一项创举。《十竹斋书画谱》的全部刊印工作完成于1633年。北大所有的这部五色套印本,刊印于明万历年间,是迄今最早的《十竹斋书画谱》。

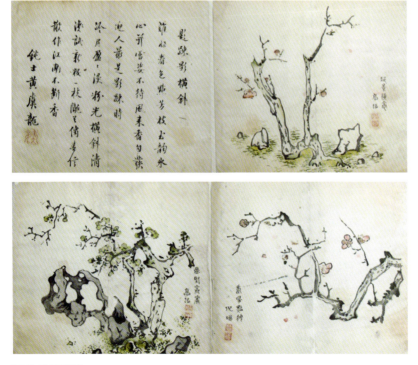

《十竹斋书画谱》
Ten Bamboo Studio Manual of Painting

4.2.12 The *Ten Bamboo Studio Manual of Painting*

The Ten Bamboo Studio (*Shi zhu zhai*) was the name of the studio and workshop of the late Ming artist Hu Zhengyan (1584 – 1674) in Nanjing. He compiled this manual as a primer for the study of ink painting. It is also the earliest manual of painting to be printed in color. The manual includes not only samples from Hu's own brushwork but also ones from contemporary and past masters. Hu intended to show the student not only the brush style, composition, and color scheme of masterful works but also the procedure of painting. The manual consists of eight juan, individually named and arranged according to subject matter; these include exemplars of painting and calligraphy, ink masterpieces, fruits, birds, orchids, bamboo, plums, and rocks, each of which has a preface by a celebrated contemporary literatus. The main process for producing this manual was as follows: first, the sections were separately outlined according to their different color schemes; these color sections were then engraved onto a set of overlaid blocks called *dou ban*; these woodblocks were then placed in the right position, and the right colors with hues and gradations were applied to them; and finally, they were printed onto fine paper made in Hu's studio. The final result of this process was the appearance of an extremely delicate and lifelike replica of a selected masterwork on paper. Hu Zhengyan's studio's innovation profoundly influenced subsequent printing techniques in China. The printing of the entire manual was completed in 1633. The five-color printed edition in the University collection was printed during the late Wangli era (1573 – 1620) of the Ming, and it remains the oldest extant copy of this manual.

4.2.13 明刻《奇妙全像注释西厢记》

元杂剧《西厢记》到明代前期已成为最流行的文学作品和剧目之一,更因书商在刊印《西厢记》读本时加入了精美的图像而受到市民商贾等读者群的欢迎,这部五卷刻本就是最好的例子。刻本全称为《新刊大字魁本全像参增奇妙注释西厢记》,弘治十一年(1498年)由金台岳家刊刻于北京。这也是现存最早最完整的绣像本《西厢记》刻本。金台岳家是京师著名书坊,这部著作附有该书坊的牌记,说明刊刻意图和书本的特色,提到《西厢记》这样的"曲中翘楚"能"吟咏人之性情,荡涤人之心志,亦关于世道不浅矣",而且"闾阎小巷,家传人诵,作戏搬演",因此需要认真对待。这部刻本"依经书重写绘图,参订编次,大字魁本,唱与图合,使寓于客邸,行于舟中,闲游坐客,得此一览,始终歌唱了然,爽人心意",显然希望此书能供行旅中的商客消遣。研究者称此刻本配图方式为"全文式插图",即"上图下文",用图像来全面表现内容。刻本共有图像273页,版面和字体也都宽大,的确可以达到赏心悦目的效果。这部刻本原由琉璃厂"来薰阁"主陈济川和"蜚英阁"主裴子英在济南购得,随后被燕京大学图书馆收藏,和庚辰本《脂砚斋重评石头记》、百回钞本《绿野仙踪》同为燕大图书馆的镇馆之宝,而最终归入北大图书馆。

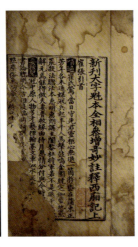

《奇妙全像注释西厢记》
Wonderfully Illustrated and Annotated Story of the Western Chamber

4.2.13 The *Wonderfully Illustrated and Annotated Story of the Western Chamber*

The *Story of the Western Chamber* (*Xi xiang ji*), which tells of the love affair between a young scholar and the daughter of an aristocratic family during the political turmoil of the Tang era, became one of the most popular literary works and plays in the early Ming. Its popularity further increased when book dealers added illustrations to printed editions. This five juan edition is a fine example. The book's complete title is *The Newly Printed Grand Edition of the Story of the Western Chamber with Big Script and Full Illustrations plus Wonderful Annotations* (*Xin kan da zi kui ben quan xiang can zeng qi miao zhu shi xi xiang ji*). It was published by the famous Yue publishing house (*Yue jia*) in Beijing in the 11th year of the Hongzhi era (1498). This copy is the earliest and most complete extant woodblock print of the illustrated *Story of the Western Chamber*. In the postface, the publisher specifically noted that this work could purify the mind and temperament of the reader, and further said that because the text was so popular, its publication needed to be treated with great care; moreover, this edition's newly designed illustrations that matched the text made it an ideal companion for travelers. With 273 illustrations, a comfortable page layout, and large characters, the work is aesthetically pleasing. This copy was originally among the most precious books in the Yenching University Library before it became part of the collection of Peking University.

4.2.14 明成化十五年（1479年）刻本《格斋赓韵唐贤诗》

李朝时代，中国古典文化对朝鲜保持着巨大的影响，加上朝鲜印刷术的流行，大量与中国文化有关的典籍得到印行。清末李盛铎收集了不少这方面的珍贵样本，这些样本随木犀轩藏书一起进入北大的庋藏，其中就有朝鲜成宗十年（1479年）刊刻的孙肇瑞《格斋赓韵唐贤诗》一卷。格斋是李朝文人孙肇端的斋号，赓韵就是和韵，这部书是孙氏对《唐贤诗范》的逐一和韵之作。《唐贤诗范》编于北宋熙宁元年（1068年），分"天文""时节""花木"等20门，收录唐人五言绝句163首。这一选本在南宋时已佚，却在高丽朝高宗时被刊刻，对朝鲜汉文学产生影响。丰臣秀吉入侵朝鲜时，此部《格斋赓韵唐贤诗》被劫掠至日本，因此上有丰臣"养安院藏书"印。但最终被李盛铎从日本搜得。

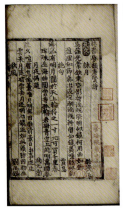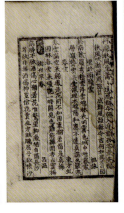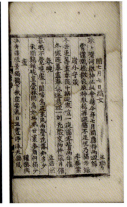

《格斋赓韵唐贤诗》
The Anthology of Poetry with Rhymes Matching Those of Tang Worthies

4.2.14 Printed Edition of *The Anthology of Poetry with Rhymes Matching Those of Tang Worthies*

Classical Chinese culture had tremendous influence in Joseon Korea. With the spread of woodblock printing in Korea, a large number of Chinese texts and Korean works influenced by classical Chinese literature were published in Joseon Korea. Well-known Chinese book collector Li Shengduo (1859 – 1937) acquired many rare editions printed in Korean, which eventually entered the Peking University Library along with many other rare books in Li's private collection. *The Anthology of Poetry with Rhymes Matching Those of Tang Worthies* (K. *Gyeojae gaengun danghyunsi*; Ch. *Ge zhai geng yun Tang xian shi*), which was printed in the 15th year of the Chenghua reign in the Ming Dynasty (1479), is one such work. "Gyeogjae" was the studio name of Korean writer Son Joseo (1435 – 1456), who was known for his literary works written in classical Chinese and its literary style. The work is an anthology of Son's poetry composed with rhymes matching poetry from the *Collection of Model Poetry of Tang Worthies* (*Tang xian shi fan*), which was a selection of exemplary five-character quatrains written by Tang Dynasty (618 – 907) poets. This latter text, compiled in the first year of the Xining era (1068) of the Song Dynasty, consisted of 20 categories and 163 five-character quatrains. The original version, lost in China from the time of the Southern Song, was reprinted during the reign of Gojong (r. 1213 – 259) of the Goryeo Dynasty and had considerable influence on Korean literature in classical Chinese. When the Japanese warlord Toyotomi Hideyoshi (1537 – 1598) invaded and plundered Korea, this copy of Son's Anthology of Poetry was taken back to Japan, and so the book has Hideyoshi's private book collection seal.

4.2.15 庚辰本《脂砚斋重评石头记》

曹雪芹的《红楼梦》最初是以手抄本的形式流行于世，北大收藏的这部庚辰本是其中很重要的一种。此书各册卷首标明"脂砚斋凡四阅评过"，第五至八册封面书名下注云"庚辰秋月定本"或"庚辰秋定本"，因此就被定名为庚辰本《脂砚斋重评石头记》。脂砚斋是《红楼梦》的早期评家，虽然真实身份不明，但与《红楼梦》作者似乎关系密切，其评点对当时人阅读《红楼梦》有很大影响。庚辰本应是八十回本，但较为完整保留的只有七十八回（缺第六十四及第六十七两回），有证据表明这是当时怡亲王府的抄本。庚辰是乾隆二十五年（1760年），其时曹雪芹尚在世，所以庚辰本是曹雪芹生前出现的抄本中保存最完整的一种，能使我们看到《红楼梦》原始的面貌。抄本中保存了脂砚斋的两千多条评语，其中不少署有年月。此本原为晚清状元、协办大学士徐郙所藏，1933年胡适从徐郙之子徐星曙处得见此抄本，并撰文介绍，才使这一本子的价值知名于世。1948年夏，燕京大学从徐家购得，后来便成了北大图书馆的藏书。

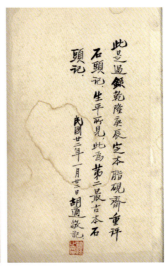

《脂砚斋重评石头记》
Gengchen Edition of the *Zhiyanzhai-commented Dream of the Red Chamber*

4.2.15 The Gengchen Edition of the *Zhiyanzhai-commented Dream of the Red Chamber*

Cao Xueqin's great novel *The Dream of the Red Chamber* (*Honglou meng* or *Shitou ji*) was initially circulated among its readers in handwritten manuscripts. The Gengchen Edition of the *Zhiyanzhai-commented Dream of the Red Chamber* (*Geng chen ben Zhiyanzhai chong ping Shitou ji*) in the University collection is one of the most significant among these early manuscripts. The beginning of each volume of this manuscript states that "Zhiyanzhai has reviewed four times the text and made the comments." The cover pages from the fifth to eighth volumes are also marked "Definitive Edition of the Autumn Month of the Year of Gengchen." Zhiyanzhai, literally "Rouge Inkstone Studio," was the pseudonym of an early commentator of the novel whose identity remains unknown. But Zhiyanzhai appeared to be familiar with the life of Cao Xueqin, or even close to the author and his family, and had read the complete draft by Cao Xueqin and so was able to offer much invaluable information on the text, such as the author's original intended ending. The Gengchen edition should have 80 *hui*; of these, 78 have been preserved (*hui* 64 and 67 are missing). The "Year of Gengchen" must have been the 25th year of Qianlong (1760), when Cao Xueqin was still alive. This makes the edition the most complete handwritten manuscript before Cao's death. Evidence shows that this copy was originally possessed by the palace of the Prince of Yiqin. In 1933, Hu Shih (1891 – 1962) discovered the value of this edition and made his finding public. In the summer of 1948, Yenching University purchased this copy, which has now ended up in the University collection.

4.2.16 蒙古车王府曲本

清代宫廷对戏曲的热衷使当时的王公贵族也纷纷效仿追捧。1925 年秋，北京琉璃厂松筠阁书坊老板从北京西小市打鼓摊上廉价购入一批手抄曲本。当时主持孔德学校并同时任教于北大的藏书名家马廉在戏曲小说史方面造诣很深，他替孔德学校图书馆购入了这批曲本。经由他和沈尹默鉴定，确认是从北京蒙古车臣汗王府散出的戏曲抄本。不久这一消息为《北京大学研究所国学门周刊》所披露。随后，顾颉刚应邀对这批曲本进行了初步整理，编制出一份分类目录，1926 年末至 1927 年初在《孔德月刊》刊出。至此，车王府曲本的价值才引起广泛的关注。这批曲本于抗战期间经马隅卿好友周作人之手，转归北大文学院，今藏于北大图书馆。曲本共 1536 种，这是出自车王府的曲本中数量最大的部分，全部是原始抄本，其中分说唱和戏曲两部分，前者包括鼓词、子弟书、杂曲；后者以京剧为主体，其次是昆曲，还有高腔、弋阳腔、秦腔、传奇和木偶、皮影等戏。曲本保留了大量传统剧本，是了解清代以来文学、社会、民俗、语言等变迁的珍贵资料。

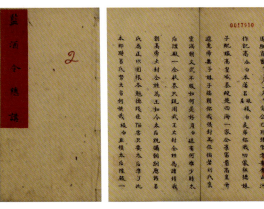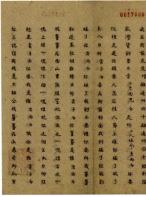

蒙古车王府曲本
Collection of Drama Scripts from the Beijing Residence of the Setsen Khans of Mongolia

4.2.16 Collection of Drama Scripts from the Beijing Residence of the Setsen Khans of Mongolia

Theater performance was a major pastime for the Qing elite in Beijing, including members of the imperial court. In the autumn of 1925, a book dealer from the bookshop district Liulichang in Beijing purchased a collection of hand-copied theater performance scripts for a small fee. Ma Lian (1893 – 1935), a renowned expert in the history of drama and headmaster of the Comte School (*Kongde xuexiao*), acquired this collection on behalf of the school. Ma was also an adjunct professor of Peking University at the time. Collaborating with another member of the University, Shen Yinmo (1883 – 1971), he concluded that this collection came from the Beijing residence of the Mongol Setsen Khans, and they announced this finding in the *Weekly Bulletin of the National Learning Department of the Peking University Research School*. Soon afterward, Gu Jiegang (1893 – 1980) was invited to catalogue the collection, the results of which he published in the *Monthly Bulletin of the Comte School* between the end of 1926 and beginning of 1927. During the Second Sino-Japanese War (1937 – 1945), with the help of Zhou Zuoren (1885 – 1967), a close friend of Ma Lian, this treasure was acquired by the School of Humanities of Peking University. It contains 1536 original manuscripts, which can be divided roughly into the categories of talking and singing, and theater performance. The former includes *guci*, *zidishu*, and *zaqu*, while the latter includes mainly scripts of Peking Opera and Kunqu Opera, as well as regional operas such as Gaoqiang, Yiyang qiang, Qinqiang, and so forth. This treasure offers rich materials for the history of literature, folk art, language, and social customs during the Qing.

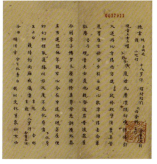

蒙古车王府曲本
Collection of Drama Scripts from the Beijing Residence of the Setsen Khans of Mongolia

4.2.17 彩绘本《镜花缘图册》

　　晚清的白话章回小说里,李汝珍的《镜花缘》是很特别的一种。故事以则天武后时代为背景,讲述众花神迫于武后之命在冬日开花,天帝因此震怒并将众花神贬下人间,掌管众花神的百花仙子因疏失也遭贬,投生岭南秀才唐敖家,取名小山。唐敖科第受阻,于是乘桴于海,寻访诸国,备历奇幻,后在小蓬莱修道不归。小山思父心切,也到了小蓬莱,唐敖不愿见女,却命其改名唐闺臣,并返国参加武则天所开的女科。小山随众花神赴考成功,得以重聚。闺臣思父,再至小蓬莱而不返。众花神则投入义军,帮助中宗复辟唐朝。小说想象力丰富,对女性的才华也尽情赞美。《镜花缘》问世不久即有绘本出现,但大都是人物绣像本,作于光绪十九年(1893年)的孙继芳绘本却是依照情节来表现,有时一回一图,有时一回数图,共两百幅图,犹如连环画。孙继芳自称是模仿明代人物画大家仇英的笔意,在大幅绢本上用工笔重彩绘制,从构图到人物均匠心独运,一丝不苟,往往能捕捉小说中最富有戏剧性的场面,加上绚丽的色彩,观赏价值极高。

《镜花缘图册》
Romance of the Flowers in the Mirror

4.2.17 Illustrated Edition of the *Romance of the Flowers in the Mirror*

Among late Qing vernacular works of fiction, the *Romance of the Flowers in the Mirror* by Li Ruzhen is unique. Set against the background of the Tang era under the Empress Wu, the novel narrates how the flower-spirits were under pressure by the Empress to make all flowers blossom in the middle of winter. This act infuriated the Celestial Emperor, who in turn demoted these spirits to the earthly realm. The Fairy of the Hundred Flowers, who was in charge of the flower-spirits, was also demoted, and so was born into the family of the scholar Tang Ao and named Little Mountain (Xiaoshan). After failing to pass the imperial exam, Tang Ao travelled abroad by sea, encountering in his journey many marvelous places and individuals, and eventually decided to seek immortality in the fair mountain of Little Penglai. Little Mountain then went to the fair mountain to look for her father, but he refused to return; instead, changing her name to Tang Guichen (literally, "female minister of the Tang"), he encouraged her to participate in the imperial examination recently established by Empress Wu for women. Reunited with the other flower-spirits, Little Mountain succeeded in passing the exam. Afterwards she again went to Little Penglai to join her father, while the rest of the spirits chose to participate in a rebellion to overthrow the rule of Empress Wu and bring the Tang to a successful restoration. This fantasy novel shows a rare appreciation of women's talents and a proto-feminist view of the world. Soon after its debut, the novel was published with illustrations, but most of which pictured human figures. In 1893, the artist Sun Jifang created 200 illustrations in vivid colors based on the main plots of the novel. Sun claimed to have adopted the distinctive painting style of Ming artist Qiu Ying with its exact delineation and enriched colors. The meticulous details and vivid depiction makes this edition exceptional in artistic value.

4.2.18 玉霜簃戏曲钞本

玉霜簃是京剧名伶程砚秋的书斋名。程砚秋不仅对京剧表演艺术有卓越贡献，也以戏曲钞本庋藏丰富著称。"玉霜簃戏曲钞本"中包含大量明清以来梨园艺人的演出台本，其中以抄录于明末清初的《钵中莲》为最早。还有许多珍本、孤本，例如清顺治十三年抄录的李渔《万年欢》。这批钞本的主要部分来自梨园世家"金匮陈氏"和"怀宁曹氏"的藏品，大都是两家和昆曲班社的演出本。也有来自于清代内务府和王府的钞本。被专家赞为"琳琅满目，梨园传本，粲然备列"。抄录者很多都是清代以来的昆剧名伶，比如乾嘉时期的曹文澜和他的再传弟子陈金雀。这些经抄录者校订的曲本常带有曲谱、工尺谱和身段谱，是了解当时戏曲表演的一手资料。旧时演艺生涯依赖看家本领，这样的曲本含独家心得，因此秘不示人。民国时期，这批藏品分别归于梅兰芳和程砚秋，才为世人所了解。其中玉霜簃藏品在"文革"期间曾暂归北京图书馆，后又归还程氏家人。2005年，北大得知这批藏品中的一千两百册重新流入市场后，用重金将其购入，使之能较为完整地保存在北大。

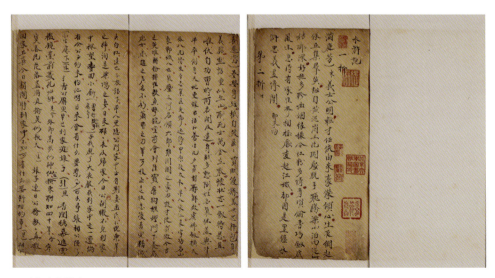

玉霜簃戏曲钞本
Jade Frost Pavilion Collection Hand-copied Manuscripts of Theater Performance

4.2.18 The Jade Frost Pavilion Collection Hand-copied Manuscripts of Theater Performance

The Jade Frost Pavilion was the name of the studio of the celebrated Beijing opera actor Cheng Yanqiu (1904 – 1958). As a fervent collector and connoisseur of valuable manuscripts of theatrical performances, Chen was known for his interest in studying the theatrical arts as well as his rich collection of valuable stage scripts produced during the Ming and Qing periods. The earliest among these scripts is the *Bo zhong lian* (*Lotus in a Bowl*), while another rare edition is the hand-copied manuscript of Li Yu's *Wan nian huan* (*Everlasting Pleasure*) copied in the 13th year of the reign of Shunzhi of Qing (1656). The core part of this collection came from two families of professional theatrical performance: the Chen family of Jingui (Jiangsu Province) and the Cao family of Huaining (Anhui Province). These were mostly used by the two performing companies and other Kun opera troupes. The rest of this collection came from copies made by the Qing Imperial Household Department (*Nei wu fu*) and the households of Qing nobility in Beijing. Many of these manuscripts were copied by famous Kun opera performers, who made necessary corrections and revisions during the copying process. The texts contain music scores, gong chi notations, and notes of posturing, and are the best sources for understanding the actual onstage performances. During the era of the Republic of China, this collection went to Mei Lanfang (1894 – 1961) and Cheng Yanqiu, two leading Beijing opera performers of the time. The portion owned by Chen was temporarily kept by the Beijing Library during the "Cultural Revolution".

4.2.19 稿本《汪荣宝日记》

汪荣宝（1878—1933）是清末民初政坛上的重要人物，也是立宪派的核心成员。他是江苏吴县人，父亲汪凤瀛也是清末官僚，以反对袁世凯称帝知名于世。汪荣宝曾赴日本学习政治和法律，归国后先任京师大学堂译学馆的教员，随后任职于清朝民政部，并兼职于修订法律馆与宪政编查馆。1911年任协纂宪法大臣，被指派为《法令全书》总纂。北大所藏的这部日记有三册，共一千多页，记录时间是宣统元年至宣统三年（1909—1911），几乎无一日间断。这正是清廷试图实行立宪的关键时期，日记中详细记录了当时预备立宪的情形。清廷授命起草的《钦定宪法》可说是中国第一部宪法草案，汪荣宝是两位主要执笔者之一，日记中对这一起草工作的过程也有详细记载。从日记中可看出，汪荣宝等人仿效的是日本明治以来的二元制君主立宪制度，并在《钦定宪法》中强调清帝享有比日本天皇更大的权力。但他们的努力功败垂成，《钦定草案》未及颁布，清朝统治便在革命中崩溃。不过从日记中也可看出汪荣宝其实思想上倾向共和。北大藏有大量重要的名人手稿，《汪荣宝日记》便是其中的一种，是了解清末政坛和社会的难得的一手资料。

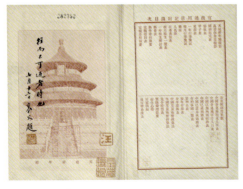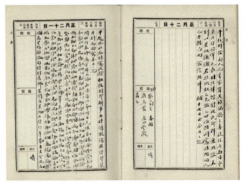

《汪荣宝日记》
Diary of Wang Rongbao

4.2.19 *Diary of Wang Rongbao*

Wang Rongbao (1878 – 1933) was an important political figure during the Qing–Republic transition and a key member of the Constitutionalist Party. A native of Suzhou, Wang Rongbao's father was also a late Qing official known for his opposition to Yuan Shikai's proclamation of emperorship. After studying politics and law in Japan, Wang Rongbao returned to China, where he taught at the newly established Imperial University of Peking and served in key positions in the Qing Ministry of Civil Affairs, the Legislative Amendments Bureau, and the Constitution Compilation Bureau. In 1911 he became Minister of Assisting Compilation of the Constitution and was designated as the chief compiler of the new *Complete Book of Legal Codes* (*Faling quan shu*). His deep involvement and important role in drafting new legal codes and the Qing constitution at the end of the dynasty makes him a key witness to the late Qing constitutional reform and political process. His diary, consisting of three volumes and more than a thousand pages, represents an unbroken daily record from the first to the third year of the Xuantong Emperor (1909 – 1911), a period most critical for Qing constitutional reform. As one of the two chief drafters of the *Outline of the Constitution by Imperial Order* (*Qin ding xianfa dagang*), Wang's diary provides detailed information about its process. One can see from the diary that Wang and his colleagues tried to imitate the system of constitutional monarchy of Meiji Japan except for giving the Qing emperor more power than the Japanese emperor. At the same time, one can also see that Wang Rongbao was sympathetic to republican ideas. Although the Qing Dynasty was ended by the Revolution of 1911 before the constitution could be implemented, this diary, which is one of many personal manuscripts of important figures kept in the University library, offers an irreplaceable source for the study of early 20th century Chinese politics and society.

4.3 金石拓本
4.3 Epigraphy Section

4.3.1 北魏《皇后礼佛图》整拓

　　北魏孝文帝迁都洛阳后，北魏宫廷在龙门开凿佛窟。其中宣武帝为其父孝文帝和早逝的母亲文昭皇后高照容荐福而开凿的宾阳中洞规模最为恢宏。石窟入口两侧有以《维摩经》中文殊问疾维摩诘为主题的数层大型高浮雕，其中分别含有整幅皇帝和皇后礼佛的场景，构图复杂而细腻，摹划人物轮廓的线条充满韵律，可说是臻于北朝艺术的最高水准。这两幅作品早在20世纪初就引起西方艺术史家莫大兴趣。20世纪三四十年代间，文物贩子将其盗卖到美国。其中《皇帝礼佛图》现藏于大都会博物馆，而《皇后礼佛图》则藏于纳尔逊艾特金美术馆。北大藏有的这幅《皇后礼佛图》整拓系清末民初时所拓。由于现存《皇帝礼佛图》残损严重，而《皇后礼佛图》则保存完好，有研究者曾怀疑现存《皇后礼佛图》的可靠性。此拓片可为其可靠性提供可信的依据。

4.3.1 Full Rubbing of the *Rock Relief of Empress Wenzhao Paying Homage to the Buddha*

After Northern Wei Emperor Xiaowen (r. 471 – 499) moved the capital of the dynasty from Pingcheng to Luoyang, the Northern Wei court commissioned the carving of Buddhist caves in Longmen outside the city. Among these the most majestic was the Middle Binyang Cave (Binyang Zhong Dong), commissioned by Emperor Xuanwu (r. 499 – 515) for dedication to his deceased parents, Emperor Xiaowen and Empress Wenzhao. On the two sides of the cave's entrance are large, multi-layered panels of high relief depicting the scene of Bodhisattva Mañjuśrī visiting the enlightened layman Vimalakīrti on his sickbed. These panels contain sections showing the Emperor and Empress, dressed in Northern Wei ceremonial clothing, leading the procession to pay homage to the Buddha. Their sophisticated composition and rhythmic lines make them excellent works of Buddhist art in medieval China. Unfortunately, both sections were removed from their original place and smuggled out of China in the early 20th century. The relief of the Emperor paying homage to the Buddha later ended in the Metropolitan Museum of Art in New York, while the one showing the Empress paying homage went to the Nelson-Atkins Museum in Kansas City. This rubbing of the relief of the Empress in the University collection was made before that relief was stolen. The state of preservation of the two panels differs: that of the Emperor has been severely damaged, while that of the Empress is in far superior condition. This has led some scholars to question the authenticity of the panel at the Nelson-Atkins Museum, but this rubbing provides credible visual evidence that it is indeed the original piece.

北魏《皇后礼佛图》拓片
Rubbing of the *Rock Relief of Empress Wenzhao Paying Homage to the Buddha*

4.3.2 《昭仁寺碑》宋拓孤本

昭仁寺原在陕西长武县，是贞观四年，唐太宗在消灭李唐对手薛举的战场附近建立的寺庙，目的是为超度双方阵殁将士的亡灵。《昭仁寺碑》即为此举而作。碑全称是《幽州昭仁寺碑》，共四十八行，每行八十四字。碑文由儒臣朱子奢撰写，对李世民个人和李唐开国事业作了极度的渲染，大有彰显李唐合法性的意图。迄今碑石尚存，但上面没有书家姓名。不过自宋代起，此碑书法被认定出自隋唐之际的大书法家虞世南之手。虽然这一认定缺乏确凿的历史证据，但书体确实比较接近虞世南的风格。北大图书馆收藏的这一本子是宋拓孤本，保存了宋拓一千多字。这一文物曾为近代书画大师和鉴赏家吴湖帆所藏，吴湖帆用明拓将宋拓残本补齐。他的题跋也对宋拓的价值做了说明，指出包括此件在内的宋拓用的是"细薄匀净"的罗纹纸，因而字迹清晰不易模糊，且"气韵温静，对之令人舒适"。

 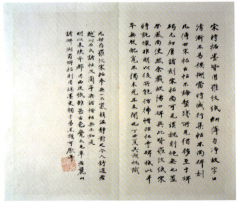

《昭仁寺碑》拓片
Rubbing of the *Stele of the Zhaoren Temple*

4.3.2 Song Rubbing of the *Stele of the Zhaoren Temple*

The Zhaoren temple, originally located in the Changwu county of Shaanxi, was founded by Emperor Taizong of the Tang (r. 626 – 649) near the battlefield where Tang forces crushed the army of rival rebel leader Xue Ju in order to bring peace to the spirits of the fallen warriors on both sides. The stele was commissioned by Emperor Taizong to commemorate this event. The text, written by court official Zhu Zishe, consists of 48 lines with 84 characters in each line. Its emphasis is on amplifying the greatness of the founding of the Tang Dynasty and the accomplishments of Emperor Taizong. Although the original stone is still extant, there is no mention of the calligrapher. Since the time of the Song Dynasty, the calligraphy of this stele has been identified, without convincing evidence, as the work of Yu Shinan (558 – 638), one of the greatest calligraphers during the Sui-Tang transition. The rubbing in the University library, which is the only extant Song rubbing, preserves more than a thousand characters. This piece was once in the collection of the great painter and art connoisseur Wu Hufan (1894 – 1968), who cherished it so much that he completed the text by adding the missing sections with a Ming Dynasty rubbing. In his colophon to the rubbing, he commented that the fine quality of the paper used by the Song rubbing maker allowed the characters on the rubbing to be displayed in a delicate and tranquil manner.

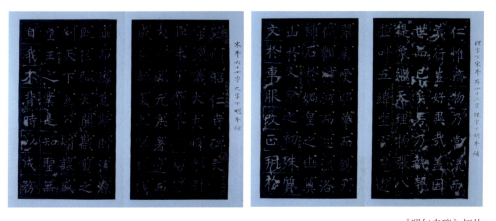

《昭仁寺碑》拓片
Rubbing of the *Stele of the Zhaoren Temple*

4.3.3 宋拓《水头镬铭》

　　《水头镬铭》是北宋文豪兼大书法家黄庭坚为汴梁法云寺而作。元祐二年（1087年）七月，法云寺在宋英宗女冀国大长公主的赞助下，建了大水镬（即盛水的缸），担任水头（即禅宗寺院里负责汲水沸汤者）的著名禅僧法秀（号圆通）请任职于秘书省典史局的黄庭坚撰书铭文。铭文在传世黄庭坚的文集里有收录，内容是："圆通师，大兰若。冀公主，舍脂泽。无量镬，慈悲杓。来者酌，闻尚檀，从智作。元祐二年七月丙子，豫章黄庭坚鲁直铭。"文字虽然简短，书法却极见功力，被认为是黄庭坚前期行楷的代表作。北大图书馆所藏的这一宋拓残本，计十六面，共二十七字，是现存《水头镬铭》的传世孤拓。

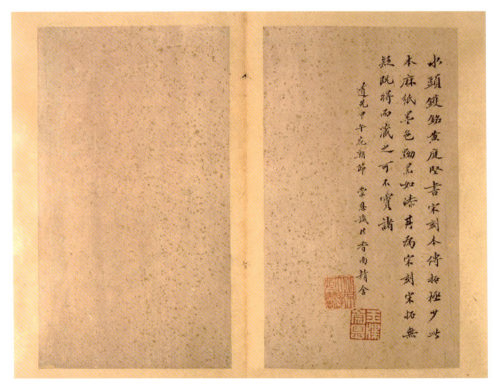

《水头镬铭》拓片
Rubbing of the *Inscription for the Cauldron of the Water Master*

4.3.3 Song Rubbing of the *Inscription for the Cauldron of the Water Master*

The verses and calligraphy of the *Inscription for the Cauldron of the Water Master* (*Shui tou huo ming*) were produced by the Northern Song literary giant and eminent calligrapher Huang Tingjian (1045 – 1105) for the Fayun Temple in Kaifeng. In the seventh month of the second year of Yuanyou (1087), under the sponsorship of the Grand Princess of Jiguo, daughter of Emperor Yingzong (r. 1063 – 1067), the Fayun Temple cast a large cauldron for reserving water. The Chan monk Faxiu (courtesy name "Yuantong"), who served as the water master of the temple, invited Huang Tingjian to produce the inscription to commemorate this event. The short text of this inscription, later included in Huang's collected works, praises the master and the princess for their endless compassion. The calligraphy of this piece has long been considered one of the best of Huang Tingjian's early career. The album of the Song rubbing collected by the University, with 16 pages and 27 characters, is the only extant Song rubbing of this work.

《水头镬铭》拓片
Rubbing of the *Inscription for the Cauldron of the Water Master*

4.3.4 白鹤梁水文题刻

白鹤梁位于重庆市涪陵区城北长江中一道与该段长江河道大致平行的天然石梁上，距乌江与长江交汇处约 1 千米。因梁脊仅比常年最低水位高出 2～3 米，白鹤梁几乎长年淹没于江中，只在冬春之交水位较低时，才部分露出江面。由于不同枯水年份的最低水位有所不同，古人注意到了这种枯水水位线在石梁上的变化，于是便在面向长江的石梁倾斜面上镌刻石鱼水标和文字，用以标识枯水水位。比如在有确切纪年的石鱼中，最早的唐广德二年（764 年）的题记说该年二月（也就是阳历三四月间），石鱼出现，"下去水四尺"。正是因为这类纪录，使这些历代镌刻的石鱼成为 8～19 世纪间该地区长江水文变化的有价值的记录，也是我们了解长江上游古水文、古航运、古气候、古环境变迁的重要资料。而这种平时没入江水中的石鱼和石刻在枯水年份又露出水面的现象，也引起历代观者的兴趣，清代的萧星拱在他的《重镌石鱼记》里说："涪江石鱼，镌于波底，现则岁丰，数千年来传为盛事。"自唐宋以来，文士游客在白鹤梁的石鱼水标旁留下一百几十则诗文题记，包括像黄庭坚和朱熹这样著名文士的题刻，可以说兼具学术和艺术价值。观赏这类题刻成为涪陵地区很别致的文化活动。北大原藏有缪荃孙艺风堂的白鹤梁宋元题刻拓片 81 张。2015 年，重庆市涪陵区人民政府又向北大捐赠了 105 幅白鹤梁的题刻拓片，补充了明清的题刻，使北大白鹤梁题刻拓片的收藏形成目前最为完整的序列。

《白鹤梁水文题刻》拓片
Rubbing of the Inscriptions of the Hydrological Records of the White Crane Ridge

4.3.4 Rubbing Collection of the Inscriptions of the Hydrological Records of the White Crane Ridge

The White Crane Ridge (Baiheliang) is a natural rock outcrop in the middle of the Yangzi River near the district of Fuling in Chongqing. Approximately 1600 meters long and 15 meters wide, it lies about 1000 meters from the confluence of the Wu River and Yangzi River. In ordinary years, the ridge is only 2 – 3 meters higher than average water levels and so is submerged under water most of the year except for the low water season between late winter and early spring. Ancient peoples, noticing the reflection of different water levels in different years on the ridge, carved images of fish on the side of the rock ledge facing the Yangzi River to mark the lowest water level of a particular year, and also inscribed words to record the events. The earliest surviving inscription, made in the second year of the Guangde era (764) of the Tang, says that in the second month of that year the stone fish appeared four chi above the water level. Such information turned these fish carvings into highly valuable hydrographic records of the Yangzi River from the 8th to the 19th centuries. The submerging and resurfacing of the fish carvings was also a source of curiosity to ancient observers. In his *Record of Re-carving the Rock Fish*, Qing scholar Xiao Xinggong remarked that "the rock fish was carved at the bottom of the waves of the Fu River, and whenever it surfaced, that year would have a good harvest. For several thousands of years this has been celebrated as a festive occasion." Among the hundreds of poetical commemorations inscribed on the rock are those by such famous literati as Huang Tingjian (1045 – 1105) and Zhu Xi (1130 – 1200). Peking University Library already possessed a collection of 81 rubbings of inscriptions from the White Crane Ridge dating to the Song and Yuan, originally part of the collection of famous scholar Miao Quansun (1844 – 1919), when in 2015, the district government of Fuling donated another 105 of these rubbings, mostly from the Ming and Qing periods, to the University. Thus the University library now possesses the most complete collection anywhere of the White Crane Ridge rubbings.

4.3.5 明拓《鲜于光祖墓志》

　　鲜于光祖是元代大书法家鲜于枢的父亲。光祖去世后，鲜于枢请儒臣周砥撰写墓志，并请好友赵孟頫书写。当时三十四岁的赵孟頫以小楷精写此志，这份墓志不仅提供了有关鲜于枢家世的可靠资料，也是赵孟頫早年书法的典范之作。《鲜于光祖墓志》原石早已不存，世上仅存两件原拓。北大图书馆藏本即为其中之一。此本虽有残缺，但椎拓时间比藏于上海图书馆的另一拓本为早。此本入藏北大前，曾为刘鹗、罗振玉所藏。

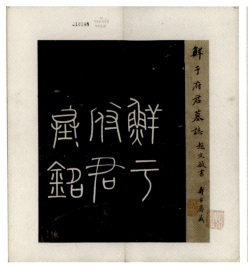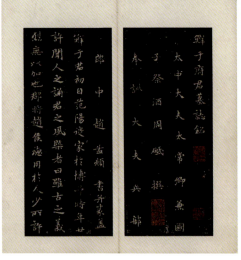

《鲜于光祖墓志》拓片
Rubbing of the *Entombed Epitaph of Xianyu Guangzu*

4.3.5 Ming Rubbing of the *Entombed Epitaph of Xianyu Guangzu*

Xianyu Guangzu was the father of the great Yuan calligrapher Xianyu Shu (1246 – 1302). Following his death, Xianyu Shu invited the scholar-official Zhou Di to compose his entombed epitaph, and his close friend Zhao Mengfu (1254 – 1322) to draw the calligraphy. At age 34, Zhao, arguably the greatest artist of his time, used regular script in small characters to write the epitaph. This work thus provides first-hand information on the family history of Xianyu Shu and is one of finest examples of Zhao Mengfu's early work. The original stone of the entombed epitaph, however, no longer exists, and only two rubbings have survived. The University library copy is one, while the other is kept by the Shanghai Library. Though slightly fragmentary compared to the one in Shanghai, the University library copy is older in terms of the date of rubbing. It was also collected by such famous early-20th-century scholars as Liu E (1857 – 1909) and Luo Zhenyu (1866 – 1940).

《鲜于光祖墓志》拓片
Rubbing of the *Entombed Epitaph of Xianyu Guangzu*

4.4 艺术精品

4.4 Treasures of Art

4.4.1 钱选白描人物图册（传）、宋克题签

藏于北大图书馆的八开的钱选白描人物图册，不见画史著录。前有"元钱舜举白描人物，宋仲温题释，憨叟题签"之签条，憨叟为明末清初花鸟画家。此白描人物图册画异域人物图像，有"女儿国""吐蕃国"等，风格明显受李公麟影响，上无钱选题识和印章，虽然不能确定为钱选所作，但接近于钱选人物画风格，待考。

钱选（1239—1302），字舜举，号玉潭、习懒翁等，雪川（浙江湖州）人。是由宋入元的大画家，时与赵孟頫齐名，被称为"吴兴八俊"之一。钱选着色山水世称盛名，今多有作品传世，也兼工人物、花鸟。他的白描人物深得李公麟之余韵，成一家面目。世传其《杨贵妃上马图》（今藏美国华盛顿弗利尔美术馆）等，有极高的艺术水准。这套册页，也是传神写意的上乘之作。

此册八开对题，为元末明初大书法家宋克的真迹，也弥足珍贵。宋克（1327—1387），字仲温，又字克温，号南宫生（此册对题每页有"南宫氏"白文印），苏州人。宋克书法受元人赵孟頫、邓文原等影响，尤长于章草，此作也能反映出宋克书风的特点。

Chapter Four: Safeguard of Civilization
第四章 文明的守护

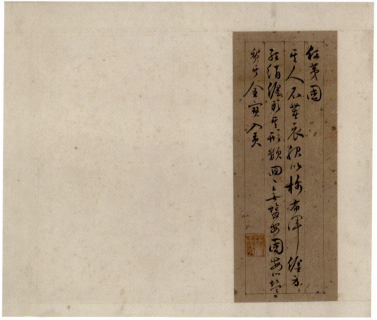

明宋克对题
Pair of Inscriptions by Song Ke (Ming Dynasty)

4.4.1 Attributed to Qian Xuan (Yuan Dynasty), Album of Figures in Outline, with Colophon by Song Ke (Ming Dynasty)

This eight-leaf album of figures in outline collected by the Peking University Library does not have any historical documentation. It opens with a colophon that reads, "Figures in outline by Qian Shunju of Yuan Dynasty, inscriptions by Zhong Wen of Song Dynasty, with a colophon by Han Sou." Han Sou was a painter of birds and flowers during late Ming and early Qing. This album portrays figures with exotic features, supplemented by titles including "Kingdom of Women" and "Kingdom of Tibet". Stylistically, the album shows

钱选白描人物图之一（传）
One of Qian Xuan's Figures in Outline (Attributed)

Chapter Four: Safeguard of Civilization
第四章 文明的守护

an influence from Li Gonglin. Although it is difficult to attribute the work to Qian Xuan since it is exempt from the artist's inscriptions or seals, the work resembles Qian's figure paintings and awaits further research.

Qian Xuan (1239 – 1302), whose courtesy name is Shunju and whose art names include Yutan and Xilanweng, was a native of Zhachuan (today's Huzhou region, Zhejiang Province). He was a distinguished painter during the dynastic change from the Song to the Yuan, as he equaled Zhao Mengfu in prestige and was grouped into "the Eight Handsome of Wuxing." His most famed paintings are landscapes in color, many of which still circulate the world today, while his other works lie in the genres of figures and birds and flowers. His figures in outline recall Lin Gonglin's hand, and his paintings such as Yang Guifei Mounting a Horse (now collected by the Freer and Sackler Galleries in Washington D.C., USA) testifies to his extraordinary artistic caliber. This album here is also a piece of similar stature.

In particular, this album has eight leaves and is treasured for its calligraphy by Song Ke, a renowned calligrapher during the Yuan and Ming period. As a native of Suzhou, Song Ke (1327 – 1387) is also known by the courtesy names Zhongwen and Kewen or by his art name Nangong Sheng (the pair of inscriptions on each leaf of this album shows the seal of "Nangong"). His calligraphy bears the influence from Yuan masters such as Zhao Mengfu and Deng Wenyuan, with a specialty in clerical cursive script. This work also reflects the characteristics of Song Ke's calligraphy.

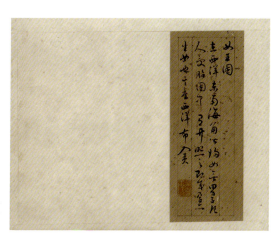

明宋克对题
Pair of Inscriptions by Song Ke (Ming Dynasty)

4.4.2 明吴彬《勺园祓禊图卷》

纸本，水墨，淡设色，高 30.6 厘米，长 288.1 厘米。卷前有画家自题"勺园祓禊图，乙卯岁上巳日写。吴彬。"下钤"吴彬之印"白文方印。因卷前有清初画家王崇简题签"米氏勺园图"，故此图又称"米氏勺园图"，图作于万历四十三年乙卯（1615年）。吴彬（生卒年不详），字文中，又作文仲，福建莆田人，流寓金陵，以画荐为中书舍人。明末著名画家，擅山水、人物，尤工佛像，今传世作品甚多。这帧手卷也是吴彬传世中的极佳之作。图虽是对勺园实境的描绘，但又不为外在形式所拘，多文人意趣融会其中。画家画石的高超水平在此作中也有体现。吴彬与米万钟交谊深厚，晚年曾住米家数年。米万钟毕生好石，吴彬曾为其绘有大量的石图，今传吴彬重要作品《十面灵璧图》，即是他为米氏所绘。祓禊，又名修禊，古代风俗每年春天三月上巳日于水边洗涤污垢、除恶祈福之会，此图即写春日水边文人雅集之事。

米万钟身后此卷流失，后为其孙汉雯所得，清初藏此画的王崇简即为汉雯之岳父。一度曾是乾隆第五子永琪（荣亲王，号筠亭）的收藏，后归翁同龢，成为翁家世藏之宝物。翁同龢五世孙、美籍著名华人收藏家翁万戈先生 2010 年将此画赠予北大。勺园位于原燕京大学旧址，今北大校园内。明末时北京西郊有两座著名园林，一为米万钟占地百余亩的勺园，一为李戚畹的清华园。勺园有山林意味，体现出文人之追求。李园则比较奢华。叶向高有评说："李园壮丽，米园曲折；米园不俗，李园不酸。"（明刘侗《帝京景物略》卷四）吴彬曾亲自参与勺园的营建，勺园图即作于园成后不久。据清顺治年间收藏此作的王崇简题跋中称："吴文中昔馆于米友石先生家最久，为写勺园图极其详备，予尝游览园中，此图诚不诬。迫甲申变后一望荒烟白草，无复遗构矣。"幸得吴彬此作，使后人览此可知这座著名园林之大概。

4.4.2 Wu Bin (Ming Dynasty), *Fuxi Festival at Shaoyuan*

The handscroll begins with an inscription by the early Qing artist Wang Chongjian—"Mi's Painting of Shaoyuan"—which gave another title to the work. This painting was created in 1615. Wu Bin (dates unknown), whose courtesy name is Wenzhong, was a native of Putian region in Fujian Province. When he inhabited Nanjing, Wu was recommended as a Zhongshu Sheren (a mid-level official at the legislative bureau of the government) on the basis of his paintings. As a celebrated painter in late Ming, he excelled at portraying landscapes and figures, especially Buddhist icons, with many of his works passing onto the present day. This handscroll is also a superb piece of Wu's extant oeuvre—though depicting Shaoyuan as a physical setting, it was not restrained by visual forms but evokes the ambience of literati mindset and pleasure. It also demonstrates Wu's skills of painting stones. During his lifetime, Wu formed a strong bond with Mi Wanzhong and even lived in Mi's home for several years in his old age. Because of Mi's avidity with stones, Wu created a large amount of stone paintings for this friend. Today, one of Wu's most important works *Ten Views of a Lingbi Rock* was indeed a painting for Mi. Fuxi, also known as "xiuxi", was a ancient tradition in March during which individuals would shower in rivers, expelling the evil and wishing for blessings. This painting portrays such a literati riverside gathering in springtime.

This painting was lost after Mi's death but was acquired by his grandson named Hanwen. The collector of this painting in early Qing, Wang Chongjian was Hanwen's father-in-law. In addition, the work was once collected by Yongqi, the fifth son of Qianlong Emperor (also known as Prince Rong, whose art name is Yunting) and was later passed onto Weng Tongsu, as it then became a treasure of the Weng family. As a fifth-generation-descendent of Weng Tongsu, the renowned Chinese American collector Weng Wange gifted this painting to Peking University in 2010.

Shaoyuan was located at the original site of Yenching University, the campus of today's Peking University. There were two famous gardens in the west suburb of Beijing in late Ming: one was Mi Wanzhong's Shaoyuan that stretched over hundreds of hectares; the other was Li Qiwan's Tsinghua Garden. Shaoyuan embodied the essence of mountains and forests, epitomizing literati pursuits, while in comparison Li's garden was more sumptuous. Ye Xianggao commented, "Li's garden is splendid, yet Mi's garden is serpentine; Mi's garden is not vulgar, and Li's garden is not disagreeable." (recorded by Liu Tong from Ming Dynasty in *Overview of Scenes and Things in the Imperial Capital*, juan 4). Wu Bin was personally involved with the construction of Shaoyuan. His painting was also created soon after its completion. According to Wang Chongjian's colophon, "Wu Wenzhong used to spend the longest time at Mi's home. His painting was elaborate and careful. I once toured the garden, and the painting was indeed truthful. Due to the Battle of Beijing in 1644, the Garden was demolished into a sight of wild smoke and white grass, no longer retaining its former structure." Fortunately, this painting by Wu Bin has offered the posterity a glimpse into this once acclaimed garden.

Chapter Four: Safeguard of Civilization
第四章 文明的守护

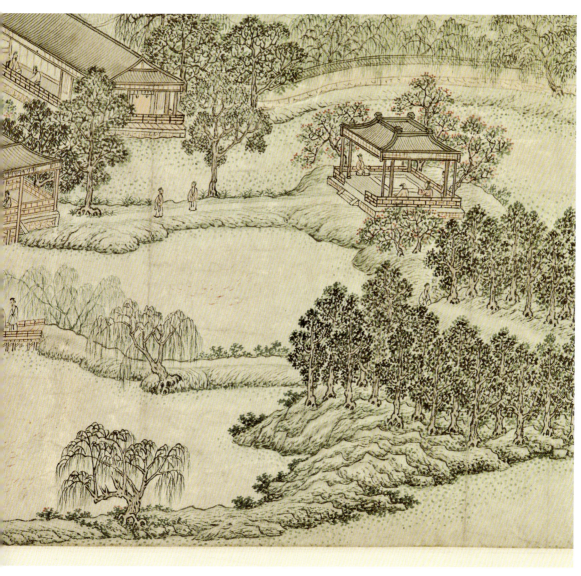

明吴彬《勺园祓禊图卷》(局部)
Wu Bin (Ming Dynasty), *Fuxi Festival at Shaoyuan* (Parts)

4.4.3 明米万钟《勺园修禊图卷》

纸本，设色，高30.6厘米，长288.1厘米。与上言吴彬之图等量。20世纪20年代，历史学家、原燕京大学图书馆馆长购得此卷，藏于燕大图书馆。洪业先生以此图为主要参考，撰成《勺园图录考》，对勺园作了详细考证。此图与吴彬的《勺园祓禊图卷》并称双璧，成为我们了解勺园历史的直接图像资料。

米万钟（1570—1628），字仲诏，号友石、湛园、勺海亭长、海淀渔长、石隐庵居士等，原籍陕西安化，生于北京，官太仆寺少卿，江西按察使。万历二十三年（1595年）进士，虽成名较早，然一生仕途并不顺利。正如叶向高所言，其意在"辋川、松雪及其家海岳父子间"（《米仲诏诗序》《苍霞续草》卷五），性萧散，着意于诗、书、画、戏曲等，尤神迷于园林营建和玩石。他在北京所建湛园、漫园和勺园，都是一时佳构。

勺园建成之后，吴彬为之作勺园全图，时在1615年，后米万钟又亲自摹之，写成此卷。此卷款"丁巳三月写勺园修禊图"，距吴彬作此图时正好两年。两卷相比，构图基本相同，吴彬为当时著名画家，米万钟却以书法著称于世，但据此卷可以见出，米氏于绘事也有不凡功力。吴彬之作格调萧散，重文人意趣，而米氏此作笔墨精细，设色妍丽，虽摹仿吴彬原作，又有所变化，也有很高艺术鉴赏价值。尤其在一些细节处理上，对勺园面貌的反映更为具体。图中连匾额都清晰可辨，清孙国敉《燕都游览志》所说的"勺园径曰风烟里，入径乱石磊砢，高柳荫之，南有阪，阪上桥曰缨云……折而北为文水阪，跨水有斋，曰定舫。舫西高阜，题曰：松风水月。阜断为桥，曰逶迤梁。主人所书也。逾梁而北为勺海堂，吴文仲篆"，图中都能一一见之。

4.4.3 Mi Wanzhong (Ming Dynasty), *Fuxi Festival at Shaoyuan*

In 1920s, the historian and former director of Yenching University Library acquired this handscroll and stored it inside the university library. Hong Ye then used this painting as the main reference to research into Shaoyuan and compiled his discovery in the Mi Garden. This painting by Mi and its counterpart by Wu Bin thus became a precious pair that served as the primary visual materials for us to probe into the history of Shaoyuan.

Mi Wanzhong (1570 – 1628) had the courtesy name Shaozhong and art names such as Youshi, Zhanyuan, the Master of Shaohai Pavilion, the Master Fisherman of Haidian, and the Hermit of Shiyin Hut. His family came from Anhua region of Shaanxi Province, and born in Beijing, he served as a deputy Minister of Husbandry and Inspection Ambassador in Jiangxi Province. He received the recommended men degree (*Jinshi*) in 1595. Although Mi had early achieved this accomplishment, his career in the bureaucracy was a difficult climb. As Ye Xianggao once commented, " Mi Wanzhong aspired to become a recluse like Wang Wei, Zhao Mengfu and the father-son team of Mi Fei and Mi Youren from his own family lineage." (Preface to *Mi Zhongzhao's Poetry,* juan 5 of *Cangxia Xucao*). His nature was unrestrained and free, as he attended to poetry, calligraphy, painting, drama, and music, with a special fascination with building gardens and appreciating stones. He was responsible for the construction of Zhan Garden, Man Garden, and Shaoyuan in Beijing, all of which were celebrated during his time.

After the completion of Shaoyuan, Wu Bin created *The Panorama of Shaoyuan* in 1615. Mi Wanzhong himself then modeled after this painting and produced his own scroll. With an inscription that reads "Creating Fuxi Festival at Shaoyuan in March 1617", Mi's scroll dates precisely two years following Wu Bin's work. In comparison, the two scrolls resemble each other in their composition. While Wu Bin was an esteemed painter of his time, Mi Wanzhong was famed for his calligraphy, as this scroll further testifies to his outstanding capacity for painting. Furthermore, Wu's creation exudes a free spirit, with an emphasis on the literati mindset and pleasure, while Mi's work is exquisite in its use of

米万钟《勺园修禊图》(局部)
Mi Wanzhong, Fuxi Festival at Shaoyuan (Parts)

Chapter Four: Safeguard of Civilization
第四章 文明的守护

brush and application of ink, embellished with bright and delightful colors.

Although Mi's painting was modeled after Wu Bin's original, it adeptly varied from the prototype and merits a similar height of artistic appreciation. In particular, Mi's handling of details reflects a more punctilious representation of Shaoyuan; one could discern even architectural plaques from his image. As the Qing scholar Sun Guomei records in his *Travel Log in Yan Capital*, "The paths in Shaoyuan are named 'Amidst Winds and Smoke'. Their entry point is an edged pile of stones in disarray, under the shade of tall willow trees. In the south, there is a slope, over which a bridge is styled 'Ribbon Cloud'…returning to the north is a wenshui slope, as a studio hovers over the water and is termed 'the Boat of Steadiness.' The west of the chamber is a high mound, with an inscription that reads, 'pine wind and water moon.' From the break of the mound emerges a bridge, whose name 'Beam of Meandering Extension' was written by the Garden master. Over the bridge further to the north is Shao Hai Pavilion, the plaque of which shows Wu Wenzhong's calligraphy." Each of these references could be identified in Mi's image.

4.4.4 清戴熙花卉册页八开

此册页八开，绢本，水墨淡设色。

清末画家戴熙（1801 – 1860），字醇士，号鹿床、榆庵、松屏等，杭州人，道光十一年（1831 年）进士，次年擢为翰林，曾官广东学政、内阁学士、兵部侍郎，余暇属意在画。有清一代，论画他不能与四王、八大山人、石涛等相比，但对画理却有精深见识，所著《习苦斋画絮》等为世所重。他是一位山水画家，绘制花卉也有较高水平。此八开册页作于早年，多得于常州花鸟尤其是恽南田之影响。境界清远，笔致雅净。

其中一开有题跋，当是此八页花卉册之总跋，言其"早岁学画从花卉入手"，后转肆力于山水。跋云："顷从旧簏中，捡得写生八叶，盖余弱冠时所作，殊嫌未臻苍古，以其尚有一种秀润之色，不忍弃去，辄漫题识数语，以俟赏音。"

此册今藏北大图书馆，画史无著录。

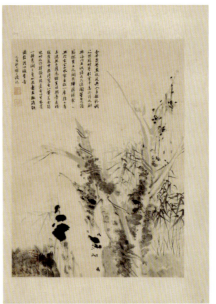

清戴熙花卉册页八开之一
One of the Eight-leaf Album by Dai Xi (Qing Dynasty)

4.4.4 Dai Xi (Qing Dynasty), Album of Flowers (Eight Leaves)

Eight-leaf album, ink and light colors on silk.

A native of Hangzhou, the late Qing painter Dai Xi (1801 – 1860) was identified by the courtesy name Chunshi and art names such as Luchuang, Yu'an, and Songping. He received the Degree of Recommended Man (*Juren*) in 1831, and was promoted to be a member of the Imperial Academy in the following year. He held posts as an official of Guangdong Academic Administration, Academician of the Grand Secretariat, and the Deputy Minister of Defense, and in his spare time, he cultivated a personal interest in painting. While he could not compete with the Four Wangs, Bada Shanren, or Shitao, he had an astute and profound understanding of painting theories. His publication *Talks of Painting by Xigu Studio* was highly regarded. As a landscape painter, he also developed an expertise in the depictions of flowers. This eight-leaf album was created in his early years and bears an influence by the Changzhou tradition of painting flowers and birds, especially by Yun Nantian's works. The spirit of the work is clear and distant, and the use of brush is elegant and clean.

There is an inscription on one of the leaves and should have served as that of entire album. The inscription indicates that Dai "started from flowers when he learnt paintings in the early years" before devoting himself to landscapes. Specifically, the inscription reads, "Just now from an old basket, I picked up the eight leaves of drawings from life; they were created when I was young and inadequate, and I detested its failure of realizing the vigorous and the ancient. But because its colors still retain a touch of delicacy and moisture, I couldn't bear to abandon the work. Always freely inscribing a few words, I am waiting for a sound of praise."

This album is now collected by the Peking University Library and does not have any historical documentation.

后 记

《燕园珍藏》出版之际,我心里有种沉甸甸的感觉。整个成书过程历历在目。自提出想法,到大纲落成,其间多次聚会商议,直至最后正式面世,我主持和见证了这本书的诞生,也深交了一批学问渊博、性情相投的燕园学者。在编写此书的过程中,我与他们一起在对燕园之美的追问中,度过了人生一段难忘的时光。

在此,我要对所有参与编写的老师们致以诚挚的感谢。无论是最初的立题策划,还是故事的精心遴选,无论是讨论时的集思广益,还是修订完善过程中的一点一滴,这本书凝结了大家的才思与坚持、探索与付出。可以自豪地说,这本书的编写阵容,集结了燕园不同领域的杰出学者,杭侃、陆扬、朱良志、李沉简、张立飞、王博、张旭东、田刚、宋春伟、谢心澄、陈晓林、胡永云、高毅勤、黄如、王杉、王仰麟、陈杰、俞孔坚、许立言、张丽娟、徐安琪等老师不仅多次参与研讨,针对各自学科领域提出了真知灼见,并亲自执笔或参与了不同章节的中英文编写。他们不仅是本书专业性的保证,更能使读者从字里行间感受到对于珍藏的别样诠释。出版之前,朱良志和陆扬还分别通读检查了全书的中英文字。此外,范曾先生欣然为本书题写了书名,王文泉、高秀芹、郑昌辉、刘梓盈、王原、王逸之、钟任建、何晋、段艳文、王宪辉及北京大学出土文献研究所也提供了许多珍贵照片和插图,这些更增加了书的美感和价值。北大出版社的陈小红和王明舟认真负责,提出了不少宝贵建议,在此一并聊表谢忱。最后,我还要提到一位多年合作的年轻伙伴杨大伟博士。他在全书组织、文字修订和出版过程中，付出了极大的热情和耐心，展现了个人高贵的品质和对燕园的忠诚与爱。我个人做事一向追求严谨完美，希望尽可能少些遗憾。书中不足之处，还请读者海涵。

《燕园珍藏》，既是对历史的尊重，也是对美好的纪念，更是对未来的启迪。每个北大人心中，都应有一份对于燕园的独特记忆。真心希望以此书，打开读者的这扇心门，留下一份属于自己的燕园珍藏。

是为记。

王恩哥

2018 年 4 月

Epilogue

Close to this book's publication, it is always on my mind what an experience it has been---from the initial idea, the outline, numerous discussions, to the final product. I led the editorial board and participated in the entire process, which allowed me to develop deep friendships with some of the outstanding scholars of similar minds at PKU. In the journey of hunting for treasures and exploring beauties of this campus, we shared many unforgettable experiences of our lives.

Here, my sincere gratitude goes to all the friends who contributed to this book, for their original ideas, careful selection of materials, insightful discussions and artful revisions. The book is a combination and crystallization of talent, perseverance, exploration and efforts of the entire team. I am proud and humbled to work with a number of top scholars in different fields, including Professors Hang Kan, Lu Yang, Zhu Liangzhi, Li Chenjian, Zhang Lifei, Wang Bo, Zhang Xudong, Tian Gang, Song Chunwei, Xie Xincheng, Chen Xiaolin, Hu Yongyun, Gao Yiqin, Huang Ru, Wang Shan, Wang Yanglin, Chen Jie, Yu Kongjian, Xu Liyan, Zhang Lijuan and Xu Anqi. They thoroughly discussed the materials in many different chapters, provided their insights and expertise, and wrote the stories in both Chinese and English, ensuring the accuracy of contents with their understanding and taste of PKU treasures. Professors Zhu Liangzhi and Lu Yang verified both the Chinese and English versions before publication, and Professor Fan Zeng wrote the title of the book in Chinese calligraphy. People such as Wang Wenquan, Gao Xiuqin, Zheng Changhui, Liu Ziying, Wang Yuan, Wang Yizhi, Zhong Renjian, He Jin, Duan Yanwen, Wang Xianhui etc., and the Unearthed Literature Research Institute of PKU provided many beautiful and precious pictures. Ms. Chen Xiaohong and Mr. Wang Mingzhou from PKU Press also provided good advice. Last but not the least, my long-time collaborator Dr. Yang Dawei was instrumental in organizing, editing and publishing this book, with his passion and patience, excellent refinement and deep love for this campus. I always pursue perfection in my life, and any comments and suggestions from readers are welcome if there are remaining errors in this book.

This book is produced not just for the respect of history and commemoration of the University's beauty. Furthermore, it is also for the expectation and enlightenment for the future. It is my hope that this book will help to open a window that is unique to everyone to experience PKU.

Enge Wang
April 2018

图书在版编目（CIP）数据

燕园珍藏 / 王恩哥主编. —北京：北京大学出版社，2019.1
ISBN 978-7-301-29426-0

Ⅰ.①燕⋯　Ⅱ.①王⋯　Ⅲ.①北京大学—校史　Ⅳ.①G649.281

中国版本图书馆CIP数据核字（2018）第060988号

书　　　名	燕园珍藏 YANYUAN ZHENCANG
著作责任者	王恩哥　主编
责 任 编 辑	陈小红　黄炜
标 准 书 号	ISBN 978-7-301-29426-0
出 版 发 行	北京大学出版社
地　　　址	北京市海淀区成府路205号　100871
网　　　址	http://www.pup.cn　新浪微博：@北京大学出版社
电 子 信 箱	zpup@pup.cn
电　　　话	邮购部 010-62752015　发行部 010-62750672　编辑部 010-62752021
印 刷 者	天津图文方嘉印刷有限公司
经 销 者	新华书店
	787毫米×1092毫米　16开本　16.5印张　240千字 2019年01月第1版　2023年2月第2次印刷
定　　　价	128.00元

未经许可，不得以任何方式复制或抄袭本书之部分或全部内容。
版权所有，侵权必究
举报电话：010-62752024　电子信箱：fd@pup.pku.edu.cn
图书如有印装质量问题，请与出版部联系，电话：010-62756370